# PULPIT CRIMES

Solid Ground Christian Books

*Burning Issues Series*

This book by James R. White is the second in a new series recently begun by SGCB called *Burning Issues*. While we have been seeking to uncover buried treasure over the last five years, we have decided to add to these priceless titles from the past, the truth of God from modern writers.

Our first title was **Yearning to Breathe Free?** *Thoughts on Immigration, Islam and Freedom* by David Dykstra. We are looking forward to adding several more titles in the months to come and encourage you to keep checking out our web site each week to see our very latest titles.

http://solid-ground-books.com

# PULPIT CRIMES

*The Criminal Mishandling of God's Word*

## James R. White

SOLID GROUND CHRISTIAN BOOKS
BIRMINGHAM, ALABAMA USA
FALL 2006

Solid Ground Christian Books
715 Oak Grove Road
Homewood, AL 35209
205-443-0311
sgcb@charter.net
http://solid-ground-books.com

**Pulpit Crimes**
*The Criminal Mishandling of God's Word*
James R. White

*Solid Ground Christian Books* – BURNING ISSUES SERIES

First printing November 2006

Cover work by Hugo Huizar
562.533.3050
hugo@hhillustration.com

ISBN: 1-59925-090-X

# Acknowledgements

I wish to sincerely thank the many who have assisted greatly in this project, most specifically all those in the #prosapologian chat channel who aided in editing, led in particular by Marie Peterson and Carrie Gambill. I truly appreciate your fellowship! To the "usual suspects," those who make my ministry possible, my wife, son, and daughter, Rich Pierce, and the volunteers of *Alpha and Omega Ministries*, once again I give thanks. Special mention should go out to Mike O'Fallon as well, and acknowledgement that Chris Arnzen is the originator of the title, "Pulpit Crimes."

I wish to dedicate this small volume to two men whose life-long ministries have demonstrated that God has reserved a remnant who honor His word and honor the pulpit. First, to my close brother and fellow-worker in the ministry, Pastor Roger Brazier of London, and second, to a faithful example to us all in life-long service to Christ and His church, Pastor Jim Handyside of Glasgow, Scotland. Both men have been a great encouragement to my heart and in my ministry. And surely Pastor Handyside will recognize these words from Burns:

> *Perhaps the Christian volume is the theme,*
> *How guiltless blood for guilty man was shed;*
> *How He, who bore in Heaven the second name,*
> *Had not on earth whereon to lay His head:*
> *How His first followers and servants sped;*
> *The precepts sage they wrote to many a land:*
> *How he, who lone in Patmos banished,*
> *Saw in the sun a mighty angel stand,*
> *And heard great Bab'lon's doom pronounc'd by Heaven's command.*

# TABLE OF CONTENTS

INTRODUCTION                                          1

1) WHAT IS AT STAKE?                                  11

2) THE KING AND HIS AMBASSADORS                       21

3) FURTHER LIGHT ON THE MINISTRY OF PREACHING         43

4) RAP SHEET                                          51

5) PROSTITUTION                                       61

6) PANDERING TO PLURALISM                             69

7) COWARDICE UNDER FIRE                               79

8) ENTERTAINMENT WITHOUT A LICENSE                    87

9) FELONIOUS EISEGESIS                                95

10) CROSS DRESSING                                    115

11) BODY COUNT                                        123

12) IDENTITY THEFT                                    131

13) WARRANTY FRAUD                                    143

14) WHERE ARE THE COPS?                               151

# INTRODUCTION

To this day I fully understand his motivations. He was an up-and-coming preacher in a large evangelical denomination. He clearly had the ability to motivate from the pulpit. He was exciting and passionate. He came to me because he knew I had some level of knowledge of the original languages. He had found a commentary, written by a fairly well-known scholar that presented in its interpretation of one of the Beatitudes in Matthew chapter five an application and interpretation he had never seen. He asked me if there was merit in the interpretation. I went to the text, the grammar, the lexical sources, checked and cross-checked other commentaries, and concluded that even though the writer was a fairly well-known man, this was one of those examples where even the best of us chase a rabbit a bit too far down the trail. The text just did not support the application he was making.

I wrote up my findings and presented them to the preacher. He was clearly disappointed, but he thanked me for the time I had taken. A few weeks later I saw that he was preaching in the Sunday morning services, which were attended by about seven thousand people, and televised locally. I was very interested when he began preaching on the very same section from the Beatitudes. When he came to the text in question, I listened with sinking heart as he made the very same claims contained in the commentary he had asked me to examine. After the service I happened to encounter him in a narrow hallway in the back of the church. He saw me coming. He looked embarrassed, looked down at the floor, then looked at me and said, "I know, I know. But you see, *it just preaches so good!*"

"It preaches good." I have wondered many times since that day just what that means. What is good preaching, and how do we recognize it? Does anyone today give a second thought to the idea that maybe, just maybe, what our God would consider to be "good preaching" might well look fundamentally different than what we would identify as "good preaching"? In my experience in the wider realm of "evangelicalism" today, the idea that there is a biblical norm for preaching, a divine standard, is almost never discussed. Instead, one overriding standard exists: *pragmatism.* If it "works," it is good preaching. If it doesn't, well, it isn't. For your conservative mega-church, it "works" if it results in sufficient "response," that is, if enough people come forward during the invitation and "make a decision for Christ." For others, success is determined by keeping the peace, not upsetting any of the key members of the church, and keeping a steady income flowing into the church's coffers. But the standard in any case is related first and foremost to *results.* Good preaching is preaching that gets human beings to do what the leadership of the church has determined is best. Preaching is a human activity with human aims and results.

I have come to view this concept of preaching as one of the greatest signs of the decay of modern evangelicalism in Western culture today. It is so blatantly unbiblical, so patently absurd in light of even the briefest scripturally-inspired reflection, that it must be a sign of God's judgment that so many can so easily imbibe such a perversion of God's truth. Do these words strike you as harsh, even unwise? I fully understand. We live in an age where right and wrong, truth and error, have become matters of opinion and dispute. The language of the New Testament crashes upon the modern ear with offense. This leads many to consider the Lord Jesus, His Apostles, and those who seek to emulate them down through history to our very day, harsh and out of step with our enlightened, if yet obviously confused, age. Error and falsehood today are excused as artifacts of our coming to understand that truth is not really knowable, and that we are arrogant if we dare forget our creatureliness long enough to say "what I am saying is right, and what that man is saying is wrong." "Yea, hath God said?" (Genesis 3:1) has become the watchword of the modern mindset that has been taught to disbelieve God's ability to reveal Himself to His own creatures. Sadly, this way of thinking has infected major portions of what is widely identified as "Christianity" as well. Believing that God is the Creator is foundational to any kind of Christian worldview. But logic forces us also to maintain that we as God's creatures are able to communicate only because God is the origin and source of that ability. A Christian worldview that does not look to Scripture for its lifeblood is a pretense.

The results of fundamentally questioning God's own self-revelation, found pre-eminently in Christ and then in Scripture, are manifest throughout the church today. Many believers are deeply troubled by the wide range of utterly incomprehensible beliefs that parade under the banner of Christianity. This is completely understandable, but such concerns flow from a basic error of thinking. They are, in fact, not Christian views at all. The Apostles of Christ would not have recognized a large portion of what claims to be founded upon their teachings today, and we show them no respect nor do honor to the God of Scripture, when we call "Christian" that which is fundamentally opposed to the heart and soul of the faith. While it is common in academia today to slap the name "Christian" on anything whatsoever that contains the words "Jesus" or "Christ" in any of its literature or liturgy, this is far from the clear thinking of the first followers of Jesus. The writings bequeathed to us by those initial leaders of the faith know nothing of partial truths, thesis, antithesis, and synthesis. They know much of revelation, truth, error, life and death, darkness and light. We will see the glorious consistency of God's revelation in His Word only as we, being led by the Spirit, think in conformity with the divine Word. Then, and only then, will we begin to think clearly about the issues that plague so many churches in our day.

Replacing a Scripturally-derived, Spirit-borne worldview with a secular one in the minds of those sitting in the pews of churches has resulted in the creation of what can only be identified as theological monstrosities, religious mutations that rival the oddities found in comic book superheroes. In the church's worship, and in the proclamation from the pulpit, this odd mixture has brought us the wild examples that we will be examining as prime examples of pulpit crimes. This should hardly be surprising. Worship and proclamation go hand-in-hand, and both are very plainly, and very forcefully, defined for us in Scripture. However, when we no longer find in the Bible the voice of the Master, we no longer realize that all we do is focused upon Him, His glory, His majesty, and how we are to be spent fully in His service. It is easy to see how these two aspects of the faith quickly fall prey to the baser side of human activity. Worship, to be true worship, must be focused upon the truth of God. Anything less is simply idolatry. Once you no longer think one can know the truth about God, that He has not revealed Himself with sufficient clarity, then worship needs a new object. Man becomes the center of worship, with man's emotions, feelings, and experiences taking center stage. The entirety of the activity now labeled "worship" will become focused upon the worshipper, with his or her comfort, mental state, and resultant "connection" to the "group" becoming the focus of the energies of all involved. The colors of the pews, the curtains, the carpet, the sound system, the kind of music, the dress, the length of service---all will become vital to having a "successful worship experience." Sound familiar? If you are involved in almost any kind of Christian service today, have attended Bible college or seminary in almost any denomination, you well know what I am referring to.

As worship has been redefined without any serious reflection upon Scripture as providing the proper norm, so too has the meaning, function, and purpose of the pulpit, the place of proclamation in the worship of the Christian church. The preaching of God's Word has been definitional of the church's worship from the beginning. The ebb and flow of the life of the church has often been seen in how powerfully the Lord's voice has been heard from His servants in the pulpits of His congregations. Many of man's religions have no place for such an activity. Christianity cannot help but proclaim its life-giving message: Jesus is Lord, repent, believe, and have life in His name. The faith promulgates itself by communication of divine truths from generation to generation, across cultural and linguistic borders. This proclamation is central to the gathered body's worship, for Christians are called to faith not just once, but always, continually. Reminder is just as much a part of the task of preaching as the impartation of knowledge not yet gained, and so preaching has always been part of what defines Christian worship.

It is not my purpose in this work to go back over the seismic shift that has taken place in the thinking of Western culture over the past generations and how it has brought about a crisis in how the church thinks. Others have done a far better job than I could ever do. But it is vital to understand that the problems we face internally today go back to particular *theological* issues, many of which are focused upon whether we really believe God has spoken or if He has only muttered just enough to get us all riled up and really confused. When it comes to the massive decline in how the ministry of preaching is viewed both inside and outside of the visible church today, we are forced to go back to the most basic level and ask a question many dare not ask: does the Bible actually define for us the substance, manner, and method of sound, God-honoring, uniquely *Christian* preaching? Or have we in essence been left to ourselves to take a vague, nebulous idea of "proclamation" and apply it as best we can to changing circumstances? If we answer that the Bible really leaves it to us to fill out what "preaching" means as we see fit, then we truly have no grounds upon which to speak of "pulpit crimes" because there is no standard by which to make such judgments. The very use of the term "crime" assumes the existence of law, a known and knowable standard, against which a crime is committed. If no such standard exists, then we can at best argue our opinion versus another opinion, our taste against another. "That doesn't work for me" is the strongest argument we can muster in such a situation, and into the resultant chaos a large portion of self-professing Christianity has already plunged headlong.

However, I cannot follow the lemmings over that particular cliff. As much as it relegates me to a minority position, I believe firmly that there is a clear, compelling, biblically grounded revelation that is to determine what "preaching" means in a Christian context. It is not culturally limited. It transcends cultural and language boundaries. It was true in the days of the Apostles, and it was true for the generation that followed them. It was true in the darkness of the darkest centuries, it was true in Victorian England, and it was true during the Enlightenment. It is true in today's confused world where every voice is supposed to have equal weight, and it will be true in the next generation no matter what worldview gains standing in the opinions of those living in that day. I believe every man who has stood to open God's Word before God's people will be judged according to His standard by the Lawgiver Himself.

Since I believe this, I stand out from the crowd today. My views are unpopular, even disliked, by many. To believe as I believe is to ruin automatically a great deal of what is considered "good preaching" today. I see pulpit crimes all around me with saddening regularity, and it troubles me greatly. I see two overarching sources of these pulpit crimes and the resultant crowd of pulpit criminals.

First, there are those who commit pulpit crimes because they simply do not believe there is any law against which they are in rebellion. Many, if not most, of these willful criminals should not even be included in the roll-call of the saints. Included in this group are those who, through their rejection of fundamental Christian doctrines such as inspiration or revelation itself, stand behind pulpits erected by earlier generations of believing Christians in denominations that once held forth the word of life. Today, because those denominations have long since ceased holding to any kind of meaningful message, they continue to "do church," mainly running on inertia. They are almost always losing members, eventually becoming little more than religious social clubs, their buildings monuments to what happens when the Spirit of God is shut out through disbelief in the word of God. The wide swath of "liberal Christianity" that denies every definitional belief of the faith falls into this category, placing men (and women) behind pulpits but in essence forcing them to do so without proper authority from God, making them pulpit criminals.

Also included in this first group are those who profess the truth at least outwardly, and yet inwardly they are seeking nothing more than the satisfaction of their own lusts and desires. False teachers may say the right things and admit that there is a standard by which we will be judged, but they refuse to live in light of this confession and instead pervert and twist God's truth for their own gain. Satan will always profess enough orthodoxy to gain an audience. Many pulpit criminals know they are committing a crime every time they open their mouths, but they keep hoping the Day of Judgment is far enough away to allow them their season of sin.

From those in this first group, we *expect* regular and egregious pulpit crimes. How could it be otherwise? We often wonder why many of those in this group even bother to pretend to own the name "Christian" or play at the game of religion. Why bother? Would it not be a lot easier, and a lot more consistent, to deny the faith completely and join the secular atheists? Yet they continue on, some simply ignorant of the law against which they sin daily, but many others fully aware of its verdict, and yet contemptuous of its wrath.

The second group may well bother the child of God today more than the first. The second group is composed of those who confess the truth that is in Jesus. They profess to believe the Bible. They may well be amongst the elect of God. But, because of ignorance of sound biblical teaching, they allow human tradition and human imagination to override the plain rule of Scripture, resulting in some of the most damaging of pulpit crimes---damaging to the people of God, and damaging to themselves as well. These men may well enter into the ministry with noble motivations. However, because they find themselves in tradition-encrusted churches without a vital focus upon the whole counsel of God, they embrace deadly errors almost by osmosis. They do what they do because it is all they know. It is not that they cannot read the Scriptures and see what they teach. Instead, the traditions they have been given since they first professed faith function as a lens through which they see all of Scripture. These churches as a whole protect their traditions and discourage any discussion of whether they have a solid biblical foundation for them. In fact, anyone who starts asking questions is looked upon as a possible troublemaker. As a result, conformity is maintained through ignorance. When you ask someone, "Why do you do this?" you encounter confused silence followed, eventually, by something along the lines of, "Well, we've always done it that way, I think."

The reason this is normally "enough" is that it is combined with another very powerful factor: if the first church a new convert experiences does things a certain way, or if the church in which one grows up has certain traditions, many will never think to entertain questions about how things are done. "Pastor Barrymore led me to the Lord; Pastor Barrymore has always done things this way; that is all I need to know." This is a very personal form of pragmatism, especially since even considering the idea that your own conversion was not the picture of perfect biblical theology might lead one to wonder about other important traditional teachings. For most, it is far more comfortable to just accept the status quo, look askance at anyone who would suggest there is a more biblical way of doing things, and move on.

The problem with the second group is that we all know lots of folks who fit into it. In fact, most of us have been there. Being challenged to be consistent in one's theology is a sad rarity today. It can be a painful process to order one's priorities and discover that things long held to be "givens" are anything but givens. That is unsettling, but for the believer who becomes convinced that God is honored when he takes His Word seriously and bows the knee to His lordship over all of life, inconsistency in the face of His clear revelation is not an option. Following that mandate may well be costly. Discipleship always is.

Sadly, pulpit crimes have multiple victims. Crimes against God's truth are crimes against God Himself. In this case, God is both the aggrieved as well as the judge (a particularly bad situation for the accused). However, the people of God are most assuredly the most obvious victims of the pulpit crime wave. The sheep of God's flock are the ones who suffer when the shepherds violate His law. The ones who are supposed to be nurtured, edified, matured, protected, fed, and encouraged, are the true victims of pulpit skullduggery. As we examine the various kinds of pulpit crimes we will see that repeatedly the precious treasures God has intended to provide to His people through the ministry of the Word in the worship of His congregations are squandered and wasted because people refuse to follow His wisdom laid out in the Scriptures. Instead of providing the kind of direct exhortation and rebuke needed for men and women to grow in godliness, pulpit criminals distract, entertain, mislead, and pander, all to the ultimate detriment of their hearers. In the case of the second group of pulpit criminals, those who often act out of tradition-induced ignorance and carelessness, they themselves are victims of their own actions. Some experience great heartache and deep spiritual turmoil because they unwisely entered into a field of ministry to which they were in fact never called. Others were indeed gifted for the task but suffered from being misled by others into God-dishonoring behavior as ministers in the church. Pulpit crimes have many and varied victims.

My approach to this issue is straightforward. First, we must look to the divine law, God's Word, for the divine standard of Christian proclamation. God has spoken definitively on the subject, and His voice has long been neglected amongst those who need His wisdom most. Then, having established the outlines of what God has revealed about the nature and place of preaching, we will examine a wide variety of variations from the divine standard in Scripture, that is, pulpit crimes, the abuse of the divine gift of preaching.

What do I pray the Lord will accomplish with this work? First, that those who have labored long and sacrificed much in the faithful work of the ministry will be encouraged and strengthened in their task. Second, that those who in ignorance have allowed their traditions to invert their priorities will see clearly the Scriptural revelation and will, as a result, abandon any and all concepts and activities that would keep them from honoring God by obeying Him in this matter. Third, that the people of God will likewise be encouraged to see the provision God has made for them in His Word, and will, in light of the general degradation of culture and church around us, remain faithful, praying that God will lift up men who will honor the pulpit, the place of proclamation, the centerpiece of worship. May God bless us as we seek to obey Him and honor the wisdom He has displayed in the divine ordering of His church and worship.

**Naming Names**

I gave serious consideration to whether or not I should "name names" in this book. It would be very, very easy to fill page after page after page with specific references and citations of every kind of "pulpit crime" imaginable, but I have chosen not to for the following reasons. First, most of the readers of this work have a computer and Internet access. A few moments with one of the many search engines would provide you with all the examples you could possibly want. Second, focusing upon particular individuals, especially when they are currently well-known, will date this work and make it irrelevant in the future. Those who are famous today are unknown tomorrow. Those who have read books from the most recent centuries know the frustration of reading a useful, important book, only to encounter names of people who are unknown to you and, since you do not know their backgrounds, the application or example being offered by the author is lost to you.

But the most important reason I have chosen not to name names is that I know the result would be a focus upon those individuals rather than a focus upon the issues I am seeking to address. For example, instead of a healthy discussion of the role of tradition in gutting biblical preaching of its power, or the importance of church membership, the discussions would all be based upon defending those individuals, allegations of misrepresentation, "missing the context," and the like. Those who have read any of my previous works or who are familiar with my ministry know I do not fear naming names. I do so with regularity, but one must be wise concerning the context in which one is working. In this context, I seek to speak to an area of massive confusion. Many active church members today have not invested as much effort in thinking about the nature of the church and the ministry of preaching as they have put into what kind of oil to put in their cars or what kind of peripherals to buy for their computers. As a result, this field is filled with fuzzy thinking and sentimentality posing as theology. To address concisely and clearly these issues without distracting the reader is my goal; therefore, I will avoid the temptation of naming names so that the general principles can speak for themselves, and continue to speak long after the individuals themselves have passed from the scene. That is not to say that the careful reader may not be able to discern a well-known name or two in passing, but the point is that the discussion will remain valid and useful long after that person is no longer relevant.

# CHAPTER ONE

## What is at Stake?

A tempest in a tea pot. No big deal. Just a matter of opinion. Something about which "good men" have disagreed (and hence, no one actually has a clue about it). All ways of saying, "It's no big deal, and, if anyone makes it a big deal, they are being difficult and disagreeable over nothing." That is how the vast majority of humanity would view passionate discussion of the manner, purpose, content, and goal of the Christian ministry of preaching, something for obscure theologians to argue about, but surely nothing of major import.

I have become convinced that nothing less than the very gospel of Jesus Christ is at stake when we speak of the proclamation of the gospel in preaching. I am painfully aware of how often strident, strong statements such as that are misused in a sensationalistic attempt to inflame the passions of one's audience, and I surely have no intention of engaging in my own form of pulpit crime, albeit in written form. Yet I believe I have a very firm basis for my statement. In fact, I may be selling the reality a bit short, since I am not using language as strong as that found in Scripture. I refer to a passage in Paul's epistle to the Corinthians. It is a passage that I confess I heard very little about in my seminary education. Despite taking a class or two in homiletics (the science or art of preaching), I have no recollection of ever having heard a discussion of this text. I confess I do not know why this passage is not emblazoned by command of authority of the eldership upon the memory of every elder candidate. I do not know why it is not engraved upon the doorway leading to every pulpit in the church. It should be, but it is not. Maybe it is because it is said almost in passing. All I know is this: if it were to be taken seriously by every man walking into the pulpit this coming Lord's day, the church would be turned on its head. The vast majority of what masquerades as preaching would have to come to an end. Listen carefully to the words of Scripture: "For Christ did not send me to baptize, but to preach the gospel, not in cleverness of speech, so that the cross of Christ would not be made void" (1 Cor. 1:17).

Have you ever considered these words? Paul was sent by Christ to preach the gospel. That alone is grounds for a great deal of discussion of the Lordship of Christ in sending His ministers as heralds to proclaim His truth, but that is not my focus here. It is the last part of the verse I wish to impress upon your mind. There is a way of preaching the gospel that, unless I am incapable of following a rather simple sentence in any language, is actually capable of doing something that is almost impossible to imagine. It is even hard to type the words, let alone consider what they mean. Could almost anything in this world terrify the heart of a believer more than the idea that I might *make the cross of Jesus Christ my Lord void?* The literal term is "empty," meaning void, useless, without meaning or effect, destroyed, meaningless. For a man who earnestly wishes to be a servant of Christ and honor Him and be used to feed and protect Christ's sheep, what could be more repulsive, more abhorrent, than the idea that in my very proclamation I could be *emptying the precious cross of Christ of its power?* But this is exactly what Paul says. Surely if the danger exists that by engaging in a particular activity I might very well short-circuit the very message I am seeking to convey, the first priority of training and preparation should be to avoid this fatal error! Yet we hear almost nothing of this great danger, this iceberg hidden in the darkness in the path of the Titanic. Why the silence?

Possibly it is because we do not readily recognize the nature of this dangerous practice. Admittedly, the Greek phrase Paul uses has spawned a number of translations. The Greek is *sofia logou*, literally, "speech marked by wisdom" or "wisdom talk." But what does that mean? The range of English translations is helpful. Here we find "cleverness of speech" (NASB), "words of eloquent wisdom" (ESV), "wisdom of words" (KJV/Geneva/NKJV), "clever speech" (NET), "words of human wisdom" (NIV), "eloquent wisdom" (NRSV) "clever words" (Broadman/Holman). I would suggest as a somewhat free, but I think contextually accurate, rendering, "speech marked by human wisdom and insight." The context fills out the meaning for us.

Paul is writing to an ancient city that in many ways had very modern ideas. It was a debauched city, with sexual license on every hand. Entertainment was big business, and if one wanted to garner an audience and make a name for oneself, rhetoric, including the use of argument and human wisdom, was important. Paul purposefully contrasts his non-eloquent proclamation of an unpopular message with the wisdom of the day. "Paul, you are going about it all wrong! Tickle the ears of the people! Get them to like you first, use a hook of some kind to gain their interest, then you can talk about the gospel! But don't offend, Paul! Use human wisdom!" In contrast to "speech marked by human wisdom and insight," Paul says, "For the word of the cross is foolishness to those who are perishing, but to us who are being saved it is the power of God" (1:18). The message of the cross is a given, defined concept. It is the message of a crucified Savior, the Messiah, Jesus, killed by the Jews and Romans on Calvary's hill. The proclamation of that message, with all it entails, is considered anything but wisdom by "those who are perishing." They are blunt. "What foolishness!" But that same message is heard in a very different manner by those who "are being saved." To them, it is not foolishness. It is wisdom, glory, and power.

It is important to fully understand that Paul was no dummy. He well knew how he could build a popular movement, one with powerful supporters and lots of money. He knew how to do it and he purposefully refused to do it that way. He knew the Corinthians would show respect for someone who would use worldly wisdom. But he also knew this: "For since in the wisdom of God the world through its wisdom did not *come to* know God, God was well-pleased through the foolishness of the message preached to save those who believe" (v. 21). God has chosen the means by which He will reveal Himself, by which He will bring men and women into a proper relationship to Himself. He has not chosen to use the wisdom of men. All of man's best philosophical attempts will fail. Worldly wisdom is a path that leads to anywhere *but* the one true God. It is a trap, a very enticing one for many, but a trap nonetheless. God has chosen a means that humbles the pride of man: the foolishness of the preaching of the cross of Christ. This is *the one and only way* He has chosen to "save those who believe."

Paul knew he was going against popular intuition. He wrote, "For indeed Jews ask for signs and Greeks search for wisdom; but we preach Christ crucified, to Jews a stumbling block and to Gentiles foolishness, but to those who are the called, both Jews and Greeks, Christ the power of God and the wisdom of God" (vv. 22-24). Please do not miss his self-confession. "I preach Christ crucified" he says. "I preach a message I know will offend both main groups in my audience. It will offend the Jews because they seek for signs. They have a particular view of what the Messiah is supposed to be, so I know that to preach Him crucified is to put a stumbling block in their path. The Gentiles seek after wisdom, and the idea that the Jewish Messiah's death is God's means of reconciliation is ridiculous in their eyes."

How completely unlike the attitude that prevails today! Can you imagine if Paul were to present this preaching strategy in many college and seminary courses today? "I know what my audience will find attractive, so I intend to give them just the opposite." He would never graduate! Today we are taught to take surveys of our areas, learn what is attractive to our "target audience," how long the service should be, what tempo the music should have, what colors most attract and have the best emotional appeal, how the pastor should dress (you don't want to intimidate!) whether you should even *have* a pulpit (it should be warm and attractive and friendly—though a bar stool is enough for most), and how long the preacher should go in telling his heart-tugging, sentimental stories before closing with affirming the essential goodness of the audience and assuring them of God's love for them. The Apostle would not have the slightest idea what has possessed us, it would seem. He knew what would automatically attract, and he purposefully, willfully, said, "No, I will not do that."

Before returning to how all of this defines "speech marked by human wisdom and insight" (v. 17), I must touch upon the text's own explanation of Paul's dogged rejection of human wisdom in his preaching. There is a theological reason, one that is grounded in what you believe about what God is doing in this world. It is one of the main reasons we have to address pulpit crimes today. Proclamation cannot excel substance. Preaching cannot be better than the theology upon which it stands. If your theology proper is deficient, shallow, and unbiblical, your proclamation cannot help but follow the downward slope. So it follows that if you essentially believe God is doing His best to save every single person equally, so that salvation is essentially a process controlled by man and his will, your proclamation will focus squarely upon man and make appeal to him as the final arbiter. It will be focused upon man, because man is, in the final analysis, in control. God has done his part, now it is up to us. And if the main objective is to get man to *do something*, all means that will get you to that objective are fair game. Play with your audience's emotions. Set them up. Ply them with subtleties. What does it matter? You've got their best at heart anyway, right? Just get them to "make the right decision," and all will be well. And so the man behind the pulpit takes on the appearance of a salesman, using all of his training to get you to sign on the dotted line (for your own good, of course).

Paul knew nothing of such a view of God's work in this world. The one who penned Romans chapters eight and nine and Ephesians chapter one operated on a completely different basis than a large portion of those who preach today. When discussing his trials and hardships with his beloved Timothy, he wrote, "For this reason I endure all things for the sake of those who are chosen, so that they also may obtain the salvation which is in Christ Jesus *and* with *it* eternal glory" (2 Timothy 2:10). Though he did not know the identity of those "who are chosen," he knew God had His people, and He would not fail to save them. He explains the ultimate reason why the same message is, to one, a stumbling block, foolishness, and to his neighbor, the wisdom and power of God. "But to those who are the called, both Jews and Greeks, Christ the power of God and the wisdom of God" (v. 24). It is God's choice, God's purpose, God's will, that makes men to differ. As unpopular as this is in today's humanistic world, it remains God's revealed truth, all of men's trifling traditions aside. You will simply never understand biblical preaching without understanding the biblical message. Preaching what is offensive to the natural man (1 Cor. 2:14) will never make sense as long as one rejects the Bible's teaching that man is dead in sins, incapable of doing what is pleasing to God (Romans 8:7-8), an enemy of God, suppressing the truth, not seeking after Him (Romans 3:11), and that the only way anyone has ever come to bow the knee in repentance and faith is through the sovereign work of the Spirit raising them to spiritual life and granting to them the gifts of repentance and faith. This is New Testament theology. The actions of Paul in Corinth, or anywhere else, make no sense at all unless they are seen in light of his own teaching. God has an elect people. He saves them through preaching a message that to them is power and wisdom, but to the world is weakness and foolishness. This is God's will. We have no right to question him. Case closed. He has not asked for second opinions on the matter. Kings get to do that. This isn't a democracy.

In the same manner, this takes us back to our initial inquiry. Paul did not preach the gospel with speech marked by human wisdom and insight. Thus, he would not make the cross of Christ empty, void, meaningless. Now we can see what he meant, and, Lord willing, see how we can avoid this heinous act of treason against our Lord. The message of Christ is a stone of stumbling and a rock of offense (Romans 9:33), and God designed it to be so. We have no right to question His wisdom, nor any right to try to soften the offense of the gospel. God has chosen to save in one way, and it is not the way human wisdom would have concocted. The worst thing about it for most is…*it leaves me completely out of the glory!* I can't save myself. I did nothing to get myself saved. I'm no better than anyone else. Grace precludes my boasting! Oh drat it all! I have to depend solely upon another? I will spend eternity forever praising Him for what He did for me? I can't claim even the slightest bit for myself? Exactly the point of 1 Corinthians 1:30-31! But that is offensive to my pride, to my ego, to my creaturely arrogance! Exactly. Well, I won't believe that then! I'm offended! I am going to go find a religious teacher more to my liking. You would not find the Lord Jesus chasing after such a person, "Oh, no, please, I'm sorry, I did not mean to offend" (John 6:64-67), nor would His apostles, nor should we today.

To preach the gospel with speech marked by human wisdom and insight is to seek to remove from the gospel the offensiveness of the cross. It is to shift the focus from the power of the gospel, which lies in its God-centeredness (the cross is how God *saves*, not how He *tries* to save but *fails* with regularity), to a man-centered "plan" that is devoid of offense for the natural man. This is why it empties the cross of its power, makes it null and void. The cross is *meant* to offend! That offense is part of the very divine power that breaks that hardened heart and makes room for a heart of flesh. It crushes so that it can recreate. When we distrust the Holy Spirit so as to come up with our own "better" means of preaching, means that avoid the offensiveness of a dying Savior, we are not only insulting God the Father, the source of the gospel, God the Son, the object of the gospel, and God the Spirit, the one who brings dead sinners to life, but we are engaging in the most serious pulpit crime of all. For God has given us only one thing that He calls "the power of God," and that is the gospel itself (Romans 1:16). When we are ashamed of that gospel so that we edit it, shorten it, shave off its rough edges, disguise it as human wisdom, we are not just showing our own disbelief. We are robbing our hearers of the only message that truly saves. Indeed, one of the greatest reasons the church today is engorged with self-righteous men and women who have no earthly idea of what it means to truly be changed in repentance and faith is because we have used a shallow impersonation of the real message to trick them into a self-satisfied religiosity that will put them squarely under the wrath of God someday. As it has been well said, what you win them with is what you win them to. "Win" them with a message that pleases their self-righteous, unrepentant hearts and you will find them to be horribly consistent within the church. They will never allow you to bring the word of God to bear upon them without loud cries of complaint. They will ever want nothing more than the thinnest gruel, the shallowest pabulum: twenty minutes of stories, a pat on the back, a smiling assurance of how good they are and how God loves them and has a wonderful plan for their lives. That's as far as you will be allowed to go. This is hardly the result of the powerful gospel of the cross of Christ.

So what is at stake? The cross itself. Just as the privilege of standing before the people of God is great, an honor above that of kings and presidents and prime ministers, so the attendant responsibility is weighty. I can have the privilege of handling the word of life itself, acting as an ambassador, communicating with clarity the message of the cross, and observing with wonder the power of that word to bring men and women into submission to the Lordship of Christ. Or, I can distrust that very message, and likewise the Spirit that promises to make it come alive in the hearts of God's elect. I can choose instead to add my "assistance" through the use of speech marked by human wisdom and insight. I can protest loudly that I have the greatest motives in doing so. I can argue that "the old ways just won't work anymore." But no matter what I say or do, the fact is I am substituting the God-ordained means with something else, and God will not honor such a proclamation. I am emptying the cross of its power simply because I am not actually proclaiming the cross anymore at all. If you edit the message, it is no longer the gospel. It is no longer the power of God unto salvation. What's at stake? The gospel. The cross. Eternity itself.

## But...

Given the current state of affairs in Western culture, a particular question, maybe even an objection, arises in light of what I have said thus far. If one has been raised with the mentality that "numbers equals success," it is very hard to get away from that idea. It becomes deeply ingrained. A faithful minister may toil away diligently in a church for years. How does one judge the work? What are the marks of real "success"? We are all human, and we cannot help but look down the street and see that fast growing church that has been around for a much shorter period of time than our own. We know the shortcuts being taken. We see the use of human methodologies. But still, that minister has a new car, a nice house. Even some of your own people have gone over there "just because." The temptation is strong. "Why is the Lord blessing there? Why not here?"

Is the Lord blessing there? What do God's blessings look like? It is a question worth considering, but we need to place ourselves in a position where we can ponder the issue outside the glaring light of our traditions and the influence of our fallen world. If we put ourselves in a position of seeing only in the light of God's truth, we will see with a clarity that can give us a supernatural strength to press on in joyful service to Christ. The question we must keep in mind is this: does the Bible give us reason to believe that it is always God's will for the church to grow and prosper in every culture at every time? The answer is an obvious "no." History tells us that when God's judgment comes upon a nation or a culture that judgment includes withdrawing the blessing of His church. A growing, discerning, healthy church is a blessing upon a nation, is it not? When God's judgment came upon Israel, did the true worship of Yahweh grow and expand, or was there a time when even God's prophet thought he alone was left to be numbered among the faithful? What does it mean to be faithful in a day of judgment?

I will not take the time to argue with those who would say Western culture is not, in fact, under God's judgment. The entire worldview permeating our culture is in rebellion against God's truth. Even the way we think is sinful, so it is hardly surprising that we kill our own young, rejoice in every perversion of God's law relating to sexuality, marriage, and ethics, and mock everything that is good, honorable, and just. So if the mighty Jehovah is removing His hand of restraint and blessing from Western nations, what should Christians expect in the church? Should we regularly see massive growth coupled with growth in godliness and serious dedication to Christ's kingdom? What does history tell us? This is not the first time the Christian faith has encountered God's judgment upon a nature or culture, is it? Was there not a period of decline, numerically, with a corresponding increase in false religion and false teaching? Is it not clear that when we see judgment being poured out (not just coming, but already being experienced) that we should look all the more seriously at ourselves and our need to remain as faithful witnesses to the one bringing His judgment and wrath upon sinners?

So what does God's blessing look like in a day like ours? Is it not a blessing to find those who will stand against the trends and stand firm in the proclamation of an increasingly unpopular message? But should we expect to see crowds flocking to such bastions of faithfulness? Or should we expect to see false religion growing and expanding so as to be a hindrance to the proclamation of the truth? Look around us today. Any clear proclamation is met with, "Oh, so *you* say, but over here Dr. So-and-So says otherwise." Every point of Christian truth is denied by some scholar, some religious leader. So there is constant resistance to the truth, leading, on the one hand, to great apostasy, but, on the other hand, for some, to a deeper appreciation of the truth. Christ continues to build His church, but what it looks like in a day of judgment is different than what many expect. Instead of looking to outward blessings, the servants of God must look to growth in godliness in the flock, a seriousness in living the Christian life, submitting to Christ, loving His Word. This kind of blessing is long-term, not short-term. It is impossible to graph and present at an associational meeting, too, but it is the kind of blessing one can look for. It is the kind of blessing that accompanies stony-faced dedication to doing what is right no matter what the cost. It is the blessing God gives to faithful servants who refuse to listen to the siren call of the world to go with their own message, their own version, but instead to speak forth only what we are authorized to proclaim by our Master.

## CHAPTER TWO

## The King and His Ambassadors

Many of the strongest pictures of God's authority and man's creaturely-ness are lost upon modern readers of the Scriptures. They are often based upon images of royalty and divine kingship, which, unless we are intent upon doing the work necessary to enter fully into the text and hear it with fresh and open ears, ring hollow to moderns who are focused upon personal rights and democratic principles. When my "rights" become the most important aspect of my thinking, God's "rights" are forced well down the priority list. The idea that God can properly use me, a creature, for His own glory and His own purposes is foreign to the individualistic Western mindset.

We rarely view the gathered body as a community of servants bound by a common Spirit, common confession, common faith, common worldview and common call to servant-hood. Church is a big gathering of individuals who have freely chosen that association and may, at the drop of a hat or a perceived slight, abandon that association. The biblical ideas of "body" and "union" find it hard to squeeze through our filter of individualism. Lordship expressed through service in the body of believers likewise fights an uphill battle for acceptance. This Wild-West individualism deeply influences one's view of the ministry of the Word as well.

It is a given that much of the conflict we find in post-evangelicalism[1] today goes back to starting presuppositions and how

---

[1]    I use the term "post-evangelical" because there really is no way to define "evangelicalism" in its historical meaning any longer. The field has become too diluted with every kind of viewpoint and 'ism' claiming fidelity to evangelicalism. When time passes, and a movement loses coherence and consistency, one can rightly describe the broad and self-contradictory result as "post-."

they have been altered over the past decades. Truths that were givens in 1900 may be almost unknown in 2000. It may not be so much that these vital truths have been examined and rejected as that they have simply slipped beneath the consciousness of a very distracted church. In any case, those who begin with high views of the Lordship of Christ, the sovereignty of God, and the clarity and authority of the Scriptures will inevitably come to different conclusions about the church than those who hold lesser viewpoints. As the focus upon the central doctrines of the faith has eroded, and attention has shifted to peripheral subjects, the foundation upon which a consistent viewpoint of the church must stand has been lost to many. Into the resultant vacuum have rushed a myriad of new ideas and practices that are, to lesser or greater extents, inconsistent with the whole of a biblically-defined Christian faith.

The role of the minister as an ambassador of Christ, an authoritative proclaimer of divine truth, has been central to the revivals God has brought to the church over the centuries. It has been a blessing to God's people to know that God has provided for a means of proclamation and example in the preaching ministry. For those who rejoice in having been brought out of darkness into His marvelous light, the fact that He has likewise provided for our instruction through the Word and the Spirit is yet another indication of His love for us.

## Our Approach

In my teaching over the years, I have come to find my greatest joy in teaching directly from the text and allowing the inspired language to communicate without seeking to enforce some kind of artificial ordering. In gleaning important truths about the church and the ministry of preaching from the text, I will begin with the Pastoral Epistles for the obvious reason that they are concerned with ordering the church's worship and preaching. Then, I will look to a key text from the Acts of the Apostles, after which I will gather together relevant texts from the rest of the New Testament to conclude our examination. I will seek to follow the author's own flow of thought within the Pastoral Epistles, which at times results in repeating a particular divine truth. This is purposeful and, I believe, useful. Repetition may well mean we need to consider that truth from different angles or that we are liable to forgetfulness!

## Preaching in the Pastoral Epistles

Ordering the church under the direction of God's Spirit: Isn't that the very heart of the frequently prayed-for "reformation" the church so badly needs today? This is exactly what happened, not in reformation, but in formation, during the Apostolic period. As the Spirit birthed the church in city after city, culture after culture, He likewise led the Apostles to order that church in accordance with His wisdom, His decree. As we read in Acts 14:22-23, Paul returned:

> strengthening the souls of the disciples, encouraging them to continue in the faith, and *saying*, "Through many tribulations we must enter the kingdom of God." When they had appointed elders for them in every church, having prayed with fasting, they commended them to the Lord in whom they had believed.

The Apostles communicated to the infant churches God's truth and encouraged them, not leaving them to their own means as to how they should be ordered. Instead, they appointed elders for them in *every* church, not just in some churches. They did not inquire whether the churches would *like* elders, or whether they would prefer a deacon board, or maybe no "church officers" at all. They exercised authority in appointing elders and giving a form and order to the church. And it is to two such elders, Timothy and Titus, that the "pastoral epistles" were written. Through these epistles, written specifically to address "church life," we are able to glean valuable insights into not only the life of the church in general but into the role of preaching and the attitude and mindset of those who would stand before God's people to bring His Word. This is as close as the Spirit comes to giving us "pulpit rules," and in them we can discern the foundations of the pulpit in Christ's church, the ground upon which we must stand today if we are to avoid starving Christ's sheep of the provision of the divine bread He would have us to provide.

**1 Timothy 1:3-5** <sup>3</sup> As I urged you upon my departure for Macedonia, remain on at Ephesus so that you may instruct certain men not to teach strange doctrines, <sup>4</sup> nor to pay attention to myths and endless genealogies, which give rise to mere speculation rather than *furthering* the administration of God which is by faith. <sup>5</sup> But the goal of our instruction is love from a pure heart and a good conscience and a sincere faith.

The first thing Paul brings to Timothy's mind centers upon *doctrinal instruction.* Paul evidently recognized the continued need, even after long apostolic ministry in Ephesus, for more apologetic instruction. The term used involves not just instruction, as we might refer to a disinterested "instructor" in accounting, for example, but "charge, order." Timothy is not giving suggestions. There is authority in his words, and they provide a boundary for what is, and what is not, proper teaching. It seems these "certain men" are *within* the fellowship of the church, so, right at the start, Timothy is charged with seeking doctrinal purity in the most difficult context possible, right within the eldership. Paul knew well that, even in the precious fellowship that exists amongst those called by God to care for the sheep, problems can arise, and men can tend to veer off the proper path in teaching.

While Paul must begin with the negative (curbing the tendency of men to wander off into strange doctrines, a reality seen in every generation and nation down through history), he does so in light of his common commitment with Timothy to the ultimate goal: "love from a pure heart and a good conscience and a sincere faith" (v. 5). Strange doctrines, myths, useless controversies, and mere speculations are *antithetical* to Christian love from a pure heart, a good conscience, and a sincere faith. They cannot co-exist. Where doctrinal impurity is allowed to flourish, purity of heart, conscience, and faith suffers inevitably.

The goal of Christian instruction, command, and order (all terms again implying a level of authority in the proclamation) is the production of Christian *love.* What makes it Christian? How does this differ from any other kind of love? It is love that comes from particular sources, sources only the work of the Spirit can produce: a pure, or clean, heart. Proper Christian instruction brings the entirety of God's truth to bear so that the Spirit can illumine every part of our lives and bring repentance and sanctification. Christian proclamation speaks to the heart, to the entirety of the believer, and brings with it cleansing. It likewise produces a good conscience. It sweeps away guilt through the proclamation of the gospel and brings understanding of the perfect work and righteousness of Christ. It continues to ground the conscience by enlightening it to the truth of God, strengthening it and training it through constant exposure to God's will and through obedience in all of life. Sound Christian proclamation produces a faith "unfeigned" (KJV), sincere, without hypocrisy. Biblically sound, focused, healthy Christian teaching contains a necessary element of charge and command that produces a faith that is consistent. Hence, these things—purity of heart, a good conscience, and an unfeigned faith—are the sources of that all-too-rare commodity, Christian love.

We must see that where these things are muddled, weakened, or completely denied, we will not be producing the very foundational Christian characteristics that give rise to Christian love. Yet, is it not the case that it is normally in the very name of love that authoritative, firm, clear Christian teaching is muted and compromised? Most assuredly. We must define love the way God defines it, and Christian love flows from a changed heart, a changed conscience, and a changed mind. God has chosen to use the Spirit-borne proclamation of His truth as the means by which He will change His people so that true, God-honoring love will be produced and demonstrated in their lives.

**1 Timothy 4:6** ⁶ In pointing out these things to the brethren, you will be a good servant of Christ Jesus, *constantly* nourished on (ESV: "being trained in") the words of the faith and of the sound doctrine which you have been following.

Here Paul provides us with another insight into the pulpit ministry, for the term translated "pointing out" in the NASB carries with it the idea of "setting before" and, therefore, teaching. In Timothy's role in teaching the brethren, he has a fixed, and sometimes unpopular, body of truths to set before them. The minister does not determine the extent of this body of truths: that is God's role. It is his duty and his joy to lay these things before his fellow believers. The preceding context includes warnings and teachings that were not at all popular then and may have resulted in frowns of disappointment or rejection when faithfully proclaimed by Timothy. Despite popular opinion today, the minister is not a servant of the deacon board or a non-profit corporation. He is a servant of Christ Jesus, and he is called to be a *good one*. Since it is Christ's command to set before the people all of God's truth, whether popular or not, he will be judged on that basis, not on his popularity.

The nature of what Timothy is to set before the people (with regularity) comes out in Paul's words, "the words of the faith and of the sound doctrine." Not only do the people of God rely upon the consistent ministry of the Word to provide to them the "words of faith and of the sound doctrine" that lead to Christian love (noted above in reference to 1 Timothy 1:5), but the minister himself cannot last long without these life-giving realities. Translators and commentators differ on how to translate Paul's language here, as the term appears only this one time in the New Testament. Many translations say "nourished" on the words of the faith, and surely this would be a good description of how Timothy was to find in sound doctrine nourishment and sustenance. However, the form of the participle used by Paul would seem to indicate that "trained" is the better translation, with the idea of Timothy being trained regularly. The picture then would be of the regular training and discipline that comes with pointing out, with authority, the words of the faith and sound doctrine to the people of God.

Seeking to handle God's Word with consistency to His honor and to the edification of the brethren, is a difficult, time-consuming task. Yet, it is to be primary in the life of Timothy and all those who minister the word of God to this day. The hard task of mastering the art of exegesis, combined with making your words understandable, compelling, and communicative, does not come easily. It takes time. Ministers should get better at it over time. How rare this is in our day! How often I hear ministers lamenting that they came out of their early training with these skills, but, because they have been put in the position of CEO/CFO/Cheerleader/Maintenance Chief instead of the eldership, they let those skills lapse and disappear, so that now they struggle to do any serious exegetical work and instead rely upon heart-tugging stories and sermonettes coupled with "appropriate" music. Just as an athlete will lose his physical skills and conditioning by losing his training discipline, so the minister must look upon his work as something that requires regular training. Of course, the result of one's physical training is the temporary betterment of a physical body that is decaying and destined for death. The result of the spiritual conditioning of preaching the words of faithful sound doctrine bears eternal fruit as well as great confidence here and now. The good servant of Christ Jesus is a disciplined, trained man who, with an eye to pleasing Christ alone, sets forth the sound words of the faith with a regularity that requires his constant attention and effort. This is Paul's consistent emphasis in exhorting Timothy and Titus, so we can be certain it was part of his training of the Ephesian elders and a constituent theme as he was involved in appointing so many of the elders of the first generation of the church.

**1 Timothy 4:13-16**   [13] Until I come, give attention to the *public* reading *of Scripture*, to exhortation and teaching.   [14] Do not neglect the spiritual gift within you, which was bestowed on you through prophetic utterance with the laying on of hands by the presbytery.   [15] Take pains with these things; be *absorbed* in them, so that your progress will be evident to all.   [16] Pay close attention to yourself and to your teaching; persevere in these things, for as you do this you will ensure salvation both for yourself and for those who hear you.

The reading of Scripture, exhortation, and teaching are the triumvirate of the proper use of the pulpit. These are the things that are to take up Timothy's thinking and time. Paul uses the imperative to press home his duty. Though there are many things that would distract him, he is to give diligence to these areas. In the original language, the three concepts are clearly connected and made parallel to one another, hence, "The reading, the exhortation, the teaching." The first term would have been understood to refer to the public reading of the Scriptures just as the readings found in synagogue worship. The Scriptures were to continue to have central place in Christian worship as well. We might note in passing that there does not seem to be any confusion as to what the Scriptures are, nor is there any confusion as to why their reading would be central to Christian worship. There was no discussion of their nature, extent, or authority. This was a given that united the people of God.

Next, Timothy is to exhort and encourage the people of God. While the elders should always be encouraging faith in the congregation, clearly we are here addressing that idea in a more formal setting, specifically, in the gathered ministry of the church. The elders are to encourage and exhort the saints to godly living as Paul would later express it to Titus:

**Titus 2:11-15** ¹¹ For the grace of God has appeared, bringing salvation to all men, ¹² instructing us to deny ungodliness and worldly desires and to live sensibly, righteously and godly in the present age, ¹³ looking for the blessed hope and the appearing of the glory of our great God and Savior, Christ Jesus, ¹⁴ who gave Himself for us to redeem us from every lawless deed, and to purify for Himself a people for His own possession, zealous for good deeds. ¹⁵ These things speak and exhort and reprove with all authority. Let no one disregard you.

Note the parallel use of terms: speak, exhort, and reprove *with all authority*. Christian proclamation is not suggestive. It is authoritative, as it must be if it includes the idea of reproving error and immoral living. It carries with it God's authority, and this is surely in line with a biblical concept of grace, for it is grace, according to Paul, that teaches us to deny ungodliness and to live sensibly! Gracious ministry does not mean non-authoritative ministry. The very idea of "exhortation" indicates that at times the subjects being addressed might meet with resistance amongst the saints, and joining it with "rebuke" further verifies this. Those with only a "said faith" in Christ, rather than a true faith (James 2:14ff), will not long endure the sound teaching to which Titus has been committed.

I pause just briefly to point out that to be "successful" in light of these Scriptural commands will often mean that one will be driving false professors from the congregation. When we seek to avoid God-ordained offense at any cost we are betraying the commandment of God in His Word. When the church adapts to the modern cultural commandment, "Thou shalt not offend," she offends God, who has designed His truth to be foolishness to those who are perishing. Once again, whether we have God as our primary audience, or are seeking to please men, will determine how we hear these texts.

Now we return to Paul's instructions to Timothy. After the reading of Scripture and exhortation, Timothy is to look to his teaching, or, as some translations render it, doctrine. Both are good translations reflective of a fact lost upon a large portion of pulpit criminals today: you can act like you are avoiding "doctrine" at all costs, you can put doctrine down as "cold and lifeless" and mock those who are concerned about it, but the fact is you simply cannot *teach* without communicating *doctrine*. The doctrine inherent in your teaching may be really bad, empty, or simply noxious, but it is there all the same. Every person who plays the "I'm into dialogue, not into doctrine" card is deceiving himself and his hearers. You will communicate doctrine when you teach. It is inevitable, and, if you are ignorant of that fact, the doctrine you will be communicating will surely be poisonous to those who absorb it, leaving them confused and liable to deception from outside forces.

Looking to one's doctrine and teaching is not merely an activity limited to a minister's training in seminary, though, once again, for many that is the extent of the process. It is an on-going, continuous concern. Even the aged saint ministering the Word will be concerned about the content of his doctrine, his teaching. He will seek to be consistent with God's truth, consistent with the doctrinal norms of the church in which he is ministering, consistent with the body of truth he has been seeking to deliver week in and week out to the saints under his care. Doctrinal inconsistency indicates either a disobedient lack of concern on the part of the elder, or ignorance of God's commands concerning the nature of his ministry. Whatever the source, such a lack of concern can be deadly to the saints over whom the elder has been given oversight.

Note the progression: "Give attention" (v. 13); "do not neglect" (v. 14); "take pains"; "be absorbed" (v. 15); "pay close attention"; "persevere" (v. 16). These are clear apostolic commands reflecting a serious concern that Timothy have the right personal priorities in ministry. You will not find Scripture exhorting ministers to be giving this kind of continuous attention and disciplined study to the many distractions we place before ministers today. Nowhere is the minister called to "be absorbed" in growth strategies, to "pay close attention" to pew colors, or "persevere" in entertaining the sheep. Instead, the focus is repetitive and narrow: doctrine, teaching, exhortation, rebuke, edification—these are the lifeblood of Christian ministry. As Timothy remains grounded in the truth and focused upon his duties he will make progress; that is, he will grow in his calling as a minister of the gospel. However, that growth can only be observed in terms of exhortation, doctrine, and stability. *All external factors used to measure the minister's growth that are not defined in these biblical categories are destructive to Christian ministry.* How many fruitful men have become discouraged because they allowed their ministries to be judged on the basis of charts and denominational "goals" rather than following biblical standards!

Do not miss the incredible statement by the Apostle that follows. After the repeated exhortation to diligent and disciplined effort in the matter of teaching and exhortation in the church, Paul states that by engaging in this difficult and daily task Timothy "will ensure salvation both for himself and for those who hear him." Contrary to modern trends, there is no question the Apostles believed very firmly that the gospel was knowable, definable, and absolutely necessary to the work of God in redeeming a people in Jesus Christ. Sound doctrine is not an optional component. The lack of discipline exemplified by so many today, coupled with a lack of faith that God has spoken with clarity in His Word, results in a lack of confidence and clarity on the minister's part, and great confusion on the part of those who hear such men from the pulpit. Instead of ensuring salvation for the minister and those hearing, the modern de-emphasis of the apostolic proclamation breeds error, confusion, and distrust. A gospel that does not inspire confidence in the God who decreed it, accomplished it, and brought us to faith in it, is not a gospel worthy of the New Testament.

**1 Timothy 5:17**    ¹⁷ The elders who rule well are to be considered worthy of double honor, especially those who work hard at preaching and teaching.

While recognizing the authority of the eldership (it is hard to "rule well" without a recognition of the authority of the office), this text substantiates what we have said above, specifically, that disciplined preparation for preaching the word of God and teaching the people of God is *hard work* when done properly. It takes a great deal of energy and effort, and it is not difficult for the people of God to recognize those who are truly engaging in the work in the proper fashion. Just as Timothy's progress would be evident to all, so in the same fashion one can recognize those who invest themselves in their preaching and teaching.

### Paul's Second Epistle to Timothy

> **2 Timothy 1:13-14** [13] Retain the standard of sound words which you have heard from me, in the faith and love which are in Christ Jesus. [14] Guard, through the Holy Spirit who dwells in us, the treasure which has been entrusted to *you*.

In beginning his second, and last, epistle to Timothy, Paul becomes even more passionate in his exhortations. Knowing his time is short, and knowing the great challenges Timothy will face, the aged Paul exhorts the younger Timothy to not be ashamed or timid, but to stand strong in the faith of the gospel. Part of walking in the spirit of "power and love and discipline" (1:7) is to be concerned to "retain, hold to, follow" the "pattern" or "standard" of sound, healthy, well-rounded words, a fitting description of the body of apostolic teaching that Timothy had heard from Paul. Paul has delivered these words to Timothy; now, by the Spirit's power, Timothy is to hold fast to them and deliver them to the next generation (see below on 2:2). There is no contradiction here to what Paul will say in the third chapter when he will direct Timothy to the God-breathed Scriptures as the source that will equip him to do everything he needs to do as a man of God in the church. Only by positing a substantive difference in what Timothy would have heard in Paul's teaching with that which is found in Scripture could such an idea be promoted. Paul well knew he had, by the Spirit, spoken in perfect harmony with the Scriptures that had already been revealed. Because of this, future generations could follow in Timothy's footsteps and continue to trust implicitly in the Scriptures, the only example of divine revelation that would be left with the church

There is a divinely mandated consistency between holding to sound doctrine on the one hand and the faith and love that are in Christ Jesus on the other. Orthodoxy outside of Christian love and faith is dead; if you love Christ, and experience His love, you will honor His truth. True Christian faith and love will show a passionate concern for the pattern of sound words to which Paul refers. There must be a balance.

The calling to ministry in the church is a precious gift to be guarded through the power of the Spirit. You do not guard something that is not in danger, and the "treasure" entrusted to the minister of the gospel should be so precious that it is natural to seek to protect it from all the forces that would diminish its effectiveness and longevity.

> The things which you have heard from me in the presence of many witnesses, entrust these to faithful men who will be able to teach others also. (2 Timothy 2:2)

This text may well be the most important I know regarding the proper biblical methodology of Christian education. While there may be great benefit in expanding upon so much that goes on in "Christian academia" today (and how it has led to so many pulpit crimes), for now it will have to suffice to note that texts such as this one force us to confess that there is a body of truth that must be passed on from generation to generation. We are not free to dismiss it in favor of something we think will "work better." Paul's ministry was to function as a template for Timothy so that the balance and focus of the Apostle's ministry could be followed by the generations after him.

Paul's ministry is also seen in this text to be a public ministry. There is no secret, hidden away, only to be discovered a thousand years later. There is no "tradition" here that is only known to the elders of the church. No, Paul is referring to his teaching, to which Timothy had been party. He had preached the "whole counsel of God" (Acts 20:27), and he had done so openly before the world.

Those things Timothy had heard from Paul: his expositions of Scripture, his teaching on the fulfillment of prophecy in Jesus, his teaching on holiness and life in Christ, and his teaching on faith and walking in the Spirit. Timothy was to faithfully transmit these things to faithful men who, like him, would be able to teach others also. He was not to alter these things. He was not to "update" these things, replace these things with new versions. He was a conduit, as the truth itself is already fixed and known. His duty was to pass it on, and to do so faithfully.

Further, he was to exercise discernment with reference to this precious gift to the church. In opposition to the normative viewpoint of American post-evangelicalism, Paul did not say, "And anybody who tells you they have gotten a warm feeling they identify as a calling to the ministry, accept, and invest yourself in trying to get them prepared for ministry, even if they can't teach their way out of a paper bag." Timothy had to know these men, as well as their character and capacities. They had to be *able to teach*, and whether they were able to do so was decided by the existing leadership, not by the candidates themselves. Many a pulpit crime has been committed by men who should never have been standing behind a pulpit in the first place.

> **2 Timothy 2:15** [15] Be diligent to present yourself approved to God as a workman who does not need to be ashamed, accurately handling the word of truth.

This text is not about how to divide the Bible up into the proper number of parts. Instead, it is yet another apostolic command to Timothy, another aspect of his duties, something about which he is to be diligent, not just for a season, but throughout his life. It fits perfectly with the theme of having the Majesty on High as the primary audience in preaching, for it pictures the presentation of the minister before God. He can appear before his Master without shame, without fear of reproach or rebuke. Why? Because he has shown diligence in the *central aspect of his Master's calling on his life:* he has found approval in his Master's sight because he has accurately handled the word of truth. The NET renders the last phrase, "teaching the message of truth accurately." This is what he has been called to do. An ambassador who does not clearly communicate the message of the One who appointed him is worthless as an ambassador. The Christian minister who muddles God's message should experience shame. However, those who put forth diligence in the self-disciplined pursuit of their high calling obtain for themselves confidence before their Master and the reward reserved for the good servant.

> **2 Timothy 4:1-4** I solemnly charge *you* in the presence of God and of Christ Jesus, who is to judge the living and the dead, and by His appearing and His kingdom: [2] preach the word; be ready in season *and* out of season; reprove, rebuke, exhort, with great patience and instruction. [3] For the time will come when they will not endure sound doctrine; but *wanting* to have their ears tickled, they will accumulate for themselves teachers in accordance to their own desires, [4] and will turn away their ears from the truth and will turn aside to myths.

If there is a *locus classicus*, a primary text, on the divine mandate for the Christian minister, this may well be it. It is found in the context of Paul's final instructions to Timothy regarding pastoral work. It is couched in the most somber of terms. It provides a divinely inspired priority list that, once again, we cannot help but note is so very much unlike the list we would create on the basis of observing so much of post-evangelicalism today.

Recall that in Acts 10:42 Peter spoke of Jesus as the Judge of the living and the dead, and that this was a definitional portion of the proclamation the Lord Himself commands from His servants. Clearly, this aspect of the biblical message was vital to the first generations of the faithful, but it has fallen out of the consciousness of a wide portion of the church today. The meek and mild Jesus standing at the heart's door looks very little like the powerful Judge of the living and the dead announced in Scripture. The Jesus of the Bible is indeed a gracious, loving Savior. Yet there is an order to divine truths, and before Jesus can be experienced as Redeeming Friend, He must be seen as Creator, Maker, Judge, and Lord. Inverting the order may save us from the frowns of men, but it likewise creates the kind of malaise we see in so many would-be Christians today. The wonder of Jesus as Savior is that, as just Judge, He could properly leave us to wrath, but, in mercy, He does not.

The charge Paul delivers to his beloved son Timothy is lodged with solemnity in the presence of God and of the divine Judge, Jesus. This is not a human charge. It is not witnessed solely by a human tribunal. This kind of high adjuration is hard for modern Westerners to grasp fully. We have lost, in the main, any sense of honoring those in authority. Even our highest public officials are regularly mocked in the media or even asked what kind of underwear they prefer! The weight of representing a high standing person is difficult for many to understand today, so the picture of receiving a charge in the presence of the Father and the Son does not strike us with the solemnity it should. Western individualism has deeply seated the concept of egalitarianism in our thought. Rarely do we experience true solemnity, especially in the context of the commissioning of one to go and represent another who is high and exalted and full of authority. Yet this is surely what Timothy would think of here. He would have seen with his eyes, or depicted in art, the commissioning of representatives of high officials, even kings and emperors, and so he would have a context in which to hear Paul's words. His mentor is giving him a solemn charge in the presence of the very Judge of all mankind.

The solemn charge to the one entrusted with the ministry of the Word reflects an understanding on the Apostle's part of the challenges that will accompany the proclamation of the truth down through the history of the church. The first priority is to preach the word. Preach it consistently, preach it to large groups or small. Preach it when you feel like it, preach it when you don't. God has chosen to use the foolishness of preaching as His means of saving His people. So, preach the word. Do not try to replace the *what* of preaching. There is only one word, only one message. God is glorified when *His word* is preached. He is not glorified when *someone else's* word is preached. The good servant will preach the word out of obedience even when his eyes see nothing but resistance to that message and when it costs him dearly. This is his task, this is his joy, and this is his fulfillment.

It is a task that demands constant readiness. When it is convenient, and when it is not convenient, be ready to preach the word. It is not a Sunday morning go-to-meeting thing. The proclamation of the word may be a very inconvenient, uncomfortable duty in the middle of a class at the university, where you know it may cost dearly. It may be a late night call on the phone. It is something for which the minister must be ready when the opportunity arises.

It is always an authoritative proclamation. Just as there is great solemnity in the charge delivered to Timothy, so too the message entrusted to him carries the authority of its Author. Preaching the word will reprove those who are in violation of its moral content and doctrinal norms. It will rebuke those who are in rebellion against its precepts. It will exhort those who have become apathetic or tired in the journey. Sometimes it will require long, patient admonition during which times the minister must cast himself in hopeful trust upon the Spirit to make his words come alive in hearts and minds that seem so slow to absorb the truth. As long as he finds joy in his service, joy in the word, and is convinced beyond all question that his Lord is glorified in the proclamation, he will press forward with a determination the world cannot thwart or dampen.

The preaching of the word, by definition, includes instruction, teaching, and the passing on of doctrinal content. Throwing a simplistic gospel presentation into the blender and warming it up in the microwave (i.e., changing the songs, replacing the illustrations, rearranging the order of the points) is not the same as providing God-honoring teaching. The minister who does not remain a student of the word for his entire life will become a cold teacher in short order, and the people of God who hunger for His truth will be cheated as a result.

Reproving, rebuking, and patiently speaking the truth—shouldn't there be a time when that will end, because all of God's people will know it all, believe it all, and obey it all? Well, that day will come indeed: in eternity. Until then, God's will is that His church struggle against false teachers (if it were not so, would He not do to them what He did to Bar-Jesus in Acts 13?), and in the process she grows in her love of the truth. That means there will be many times in her experience where "truth has stumbled in the street" (Isaiah 59:14), and the majority of the minister's audience will be seeking their own desires. They will have no desire for truth, and lonely will be the man who doggedly remains faithful thereto! The first thing to go is patient endurance of sound doctrine. Why would sound doctrine bother anyone? It is because sound doctrine always points to a holy God and exposes sinful men. Sound doctrine does not pander to selfish desires or hip trends. It calls men to self-denial and godly living, repentance, and submission. Those who remain unrepentant squirm under sound doctrine, as it is bothersome and offensive to them. Once you get enough malcontents together, they will not "endure" it.

Paul's description of religious hypocrisy has proven itself over and over again throughout history. Why do people bother with religion when they really have no desire to be submitted to God or allow any change to take place in their lives? It is hard to say, but evidently there are enough of them to put together entire religions. They want to maintain an outward show of religion, so they go shopping for religious teachers. They want to have their ears tickled. They do not want life-changing truth. They do not want to hear about holiness or anything like it. They want to have their emotions stirred and their consciences soothed. They want to be told "everything is alright." Whatever else they will put up with, they cannot stand orthodoxy. If it is what was believed before, well, we all know that can't be right (because, if it is, I need to change and repent!).

As the New English Translation puts it, "they have an insatiable curiosity to hear new things." And when in the market to find teachers to tell them new things, they will find a large number of folks applying for the job. They will collect false teachers like boys collect baseball cards. All of this is but a cover as they purposefully and knowingly turn their ears away from the truth. The truth is offensive to them. They have no heart for it. The minister who is preaching the word faithfully is the last person on the planet they want to be around. So, being religious people, they have a void inside which they vainly try to fill with myths and falsehoods.

We live in a day where we see this all around us. Falsehood abounds. Apostasy is on every corner. How should the godly minister react to these things? He knows that if he is faithful to God-breathed Scripture he will face all sorts of trials and difficulties. He can see the church down the road doing so much better by avoiding all the "hard" portions of Scripture. Again, the Apostle's words ring clear, "But you, be sober in all things, endure hardship, do the work of an evangelist, fulfill your ministry" (v. 5). In contrast to those pandering to the unregenerate religious, Timothy is to remain sober, vigilant, endure hardship, press forward, proclaim, proclaim, proclaim. Do not be envious of their physical comforts, for they are perishing. Stay focused upon the eternal prize.

### Titus, Ministering on Crete

> **Titus 1:5-11** ⁵ For this reason I left you in Crete, that you would set in order what remains and appoint elders in every city as I directed you, ⁶ *namely*, if any man is above reproach, the husband of one wife, having children who believe, not accused of dissipation or rebellion. ⁷ For the overseer must be above reproach as God's steward, not self-willed, not quick-tempered, not addicted to wine, not pugnacious, not fond of sordid gain, ⁸ but hospitable, loving what is good, sensible, just, devout, self-controlled, ⁹ holding fast the faithful word which is in accordance with the teaching, so that he will be able both to exhort in sound doctrine and to refute those who contradict. ¹⁰ For there are many rebellious men, empty talkers and deceivers, especially those of the circumcision, ¹¹ who must be silenced because they are upsetting whole families, teaching things they should not *teach* for the sake of sordid gain.

The qualifications for elders found here (and in 1 Timothy 3) are a gold-mine of vital information regarding the order Christ has provided to the structure and functioning of His church, and there is a strong temptation to examine each element of this text. Instead, we need to look at what we can learn from these qualifications and how they help us to avoid committing pulpit crimes. *A large portion of pulpit crime is due to ignoring these God-given standards.*

Titus was setting the church in order. There is a form to the church. Part of that plan involves the appointment and continuation of elders in the local churches. Paul lays out the qualifications for those men who are to be chosen as elders (plural!). Titus is given the charge to examine these men. Elders are not self-chosen. They are chosen from outside themselves on the basis of particular qualifications. In many portions of post-evangelicalism today, any man can claim a "call" and "enter the ministry," and no one is to say a negative word lest they "question" the Holy Spirit. Yet, this is not a biblical view. Serious examination of men on the basis of these qualifications is a must for the church.

The elder is God's steward, entrusted (note the constant emphasis upon this) with the precious word of truth. He must hold fast, in the midst of opposition, the faithful word in accordance with sound doctrine. Without this foundation, he will not be able to exhort and refute, i.e. look inward (exhort, encourage, warn) and outward (refute, engage in apologetic defense of the faith). The outward may, at times, look like it is "inward," for the "rebellious men" (same root term used in 1:6 of rebellious children---people who refuse proper authority and go out on their own) are normally false teachers within what appears to the outside world as "the church." This is an issue even more prevalent in our situation today than it was in the primitive church. These men must be silenced and not given a platform for teaching within the church. They teach what they teach "for the sake of sordid gain." Could there be any more accurate description of the state of affairs we see in the church today? Could it be made any clearer that sound theology, teaching ability, even apologetic capacity, are part of the Spirit's gifting of men who are to function as elders in the flock of Christ? Does it not follow just as inevitably that, when the church embraces theologies and viewpoints that preclude such teaching and apologetic endeavor, she is only hurting herself and her flock? Christ will bless His people when they submit to His lordship and follow His commands. He has revealed His standards. We dare not think ourselves wiser than He.

When we compare 1 Timothy 3 with Titus 1, we can produce a fairly full list of qualifications used by the Apostle Paul. The fact that these lists are only relevant to men has, for many centuries, been taken as clear evidence that women were not placed in the position of eldership in the early church. There can hardly be any argument of that fact. Today we are told that this was all just cultural and thus cannot derive any kind of norm from the absence of women elders in the apostolic ministry. Aside from the fact that the apostolic ministry broke all sorts of "cultural norms" as it is, we would still be left wondering how we are to derive apostolic qualifications for women when the Apostles left us no guidance on the issue. Do we just apply these same standards but drop the gender-specific elements? Or should we see a consistency between these lists and other texts, such as 1 Timothy 2:12? We will later address this issue and the many pulpit crimes related to it.

> **Titus 2:1** But as for you, speak the things which are fitting for sound doctrine.

When the Apostle says, "but as for you," he is normally contrasting the truth-speaking minister of the gospel to others, and that is the case here as well. Immediately before, Paul referred to those who "profess to know God, but by *their* deeds they deny *Him*, being detestable and disobedient and worthless for any good deed." In contrast to these *religious* men who, while professing faith, deny its reality, Titus is to...*speak things fitting for sound doctrine!* What a contrast, since, for most today, the concept of sound doctrine would hardly be the first thing they would consider to be the contrast to false and empty profession! Paul knows speaking God's truth consistently is always costly, and sound doctrine walks hand-in-hand with dedication to the truth. So, we are given what might be called a filter, a lens, a guide. We want to communicate sound doctrine to the flock. What will help us do so, and, just as importantly, what will hinder that communication? If our highest goal is the edification of the saints, this will impact how we order the service and where we place our priorities.

> **Titus 2:7-8**  7 in all things show yourself to be an example of good deeds, *with* purity in doctrine, dignified,  8 sound *in* speech which is beyond reproach, so that the opponent will be put to shame, having nothing bad to say about us.

It is not easy to be a model for the sheep. Every elder falters repeatedly and he is always seeking grace for the task. In our context, Titus is exhorted to model his life in such a fashion that he displays *purity in doctrine.* Literally, it means, "in your teaching, pure," or "sound." God simply is not honored by muddled theology. If you teach one thing about God, something contradictory about Christ, and something else altogether about salvation, how can the people of God come to a clear knowledge of the truth? It is the elder's duty to be pure, consistent, and non-contradictory in his teaching. Does that take work, thought, and diligent study throughout one's life? Yes, it does. That is his calling, and God gifts him to the task and makes it something that brings joy to his heart.

Likewise, Titus is to be dignified in his comportment and behavior before the people of God. Dignified does not mean dead, boring, or stiff. However, it does mean having a sense of being in the presence of God and representing His truth. It does mean honoring the truth and rejecting worldliness.

Being sound in speech would mean giving careful consideration to how one uses the tongue. A person who is sound in speech is honest and does not engage in hysterics or sensationalism. When people do not guard their tongues, they give the enemy grounds for accusation.

> **Titus 3:8-9**  8 This is a trustworthy statement; and concerning these things I want you to speak confidently, so that those who have believed God will be careful to engage in good deeds. These things are good and profitable for men.  9 But avoid foolish controversies and genealogies and strife and disputes about the Law, for they are unprofitable and worthless.

How can the man of God speak confidently in a day of doubt and controversy? He can do so when the Spirit of God convinces him of the gospel and his standing in Christ. When he gives forth a clear message, the foundation is laid for the people of God to live as

God intends them to live, engaging in good works. When the message becomes muddled and distracted by useless controversies that do not speak to the heart of the faith, that foundation is lost. How important is the minister's discipline, focus, and discernment! Preaching without power, confidence, and certainty does not lead true believers to be "careful to engage in good deeds."

# CHAPTER THREE

## Further Light on the Ministry of Preaching

### Christ, Faith, Word, Spirit

**Acts 10:42** "And He ordered us to preach to the people, and solemnly to testify that this is the One who has been appointed by God as Judge of the living and the dead."

Peter is proclaiming the gospel to Cornelius and his household, and as he does so, he makes mention of the divine authority that stands behind his preaching. Christ, to whom all authority in heaven and earth has been given (Matthew 28:18), commands His followers to preach. It is not an optional activity. It is not, "Well, if it is convenient, we will invest a little effort." It is a command of Christ to His church, a divine imperative. There are not many activities defined for the church where it can be said with certainty, "Christ ordered us to engage in this," but this can and must be said of preaching.

In this context, preaching "to the people" had a particular meaning. Those doing the preaching knew there would be resistance and a cost (John 9:22). This was due to the content of the message. To proclaim the One crucified by the Jewish leaders in Jerusalem as the "One appointed by God as Judge of the living and the dead" was to take a stand that admitted no compromise. Anyone who would knowingly confess Christ in this manner was taking a definitive step with lasting results. Given that this is a command, obviously those fulfilling the command could not choose to edit, alter, or soften the message itself. It was an all-or-nothing message. They were not testifying that Jesus *might be* the Judge of the living and the dead.

They were not testifying that Jesus was the Judge of some of the living and some of the dead, either. This was a message that was directed at each and every person in whatever audience they addressed (since, we would assume, everyone fits into the two rather all-encompassing categories of the "living" and the "dead").

Note as well that proclaiming Jesus as the Judge of the living and the dead is not quite the same thing as saying Jesus will be your best buddy. It is not the same as saying believing in Jesus will fix your financial woes, straighten your teeth, and improve your marriage. In fact, accurately identifying Jesus as each person's *judge* is anything but attractive. Furthermore, outside of the work of the Spirit of God in a person's heart, *this message will repel.* Think of it: "Hello, Mr. Criminal. You know you are guilty, and here comes the judge."

This message was delivered in the form of a *testimony*. We bear witness to these things. "I swear that this is true. I've experienced it myself. I have acknowledged Jesus to be the Judge of the living and the dead, and I have put my faith in Him so as to receive forgiveness of sins." By testifying, we are putting ourselves on the line as a matter of integrity, but we are also joining our audience as fellow sinners in need of grace and forgiveness. It is only as the redeemed that we point others to the Redeemer, as those forgiven testifying to the source of forgiveness.

Finally, there is a key term used here that has been lost in the large portion of preaching and proclamation today, one we saw in Paul's instructions to Timothy and Titus: *solemnity.* This is actually part of the term "to testify." Our testimony is to be solemn, serious, and befitting the subject of proclamation. There is something unnatural about speaking of eternal judgment, redemption, forgiveness, lordship, and life in the context of light-hearted entertainment and Hawaiian shirt informality. I'm sorry, but it is hard for me to take a man seriously who rides a Harley into the sanctuary, for example, (nothing wrong in riding one *to* the service!) or who is going out of his way to be viewed not as a herald of a majestic person with a weighty message, but as my buddy, my pal, my next door neighbor. This kind of seriousness, fervency, and gravity is not inconsistent with the joy that marks one's own testimony of redemption and forgiveness. It does not mean that one's proclamation has to be boring, stiff, or lacking in interest or even appropriate humor. Sadly, we live in a day when many who come into the fellowship lack basic listening skills or the discipline to pay attention for almost any length of time at all. An appropriate, topic-sensitive use of humor can "refocus" an audience so that one can press home an important statement. However, humor can never become the vehicle of real Christian preaching. When we testify that Jesus is the Judge of the living and the dead, that is not a joking matter. One cannot but speak of such weighty matters with a solemnity fitting the subject.

> **Acts 20:24-32** 24 "But I do not consider my life of any account as dear to myself, so that I may finish my course and the ministry which I received from the Lord Jesus, to testify solemnly of the gospel of the grace of God. 25 "And now, behold, I know that all of you, among whom I went about preaching the kingdom, will no longer see my face. 26 "Therefore, I testify to you this day that I am innocent of the blood of all men. 27 "For I did not shrink from declaring to you the whole purpose of God. 28 "Be on guard for yourselves and for all the flock, among which the Holy Spirit has made you overseers, to shepherd the church of God which He purchased with His own blood. 29 "I know that after my departure savage wolves will come in among you, not sparing the flock; 30 and from among your own selves men will arise, speaking perverse things, to draw away the disciples after them. 31 "Therefore be on the alert, remembering that night and day for a period of three years I did not cease to admonish each one with tears. 32 "And now I commend you to God and to the word of His grace, which is able to build *you* up and to give *you* the inheritance among all those who are sanctified.

For many ministers of the gospel, this, together with some of the pastoral epistle texts, provides the very charter of our ministry. Its depth and personal passion speak to anyone into whose bones the Spirit has placed the desire to proclaim God's truth. The Apostle sees the call of ministry as all-consuming, definitional of every aspect of his earthly life. He has received this ministry from the Lord Jesus. He did not pursue it, seek it, or covet it. It is a gift, a race he must run to the glory of Christ.

We see again the concept of solemn testimony. He is to testify of the gospel. It is a reality to him, and he testifies to others that they stand in need of the gospel of the grace of God. To testify often had legal connotations, and so it speaks to the seriousness of the proclamation. You are speaking of matters of truth. This is not just your opinion. It is not just your feelings. This gospel does not depend upon you for its validity, its power, or its reality. You testify to something that God has done.

Because of the nature of the gospel, Paul describes his testimony as "solemn." There is a commensurate seriousness in the means by which he makes known what God has done in Christ. Any person who stands solely by the grace of God cannot be anything but solemn in testifying to that reality.

The solemnity of his calling has likewise caused him to be full in his exposition of God's truth so that, with a clear conscience, he can claim to be innocent of the blood of all men. Why? He did not fear the face of men. He knew himself to be the representative of another; he knew the content of his message was not his to determine or define. Therefore, he did not "shrink from" or "shun" declaring the "whole counsel of God." Why would there be reason to shrink back anyway, unless, of course, there were major portions of God's purpose that are *offensive* to the natural man? And even in the context of the church, every minister knows there are those divine truths that will cause him no end of grief and will raise the resistance of some. It is much easier to present a nice, grandfatherly picture of God that will not challenge anyone than it is to present the sovereign King of the Universe revealed in Scripture. It is so much easier to proclaim *part* of the counsel of God rather than the whole.

This places a dreadful weight upon the head of the one entrusted with the message itself. If an ambassador decides to edit down the message he is to deliver, he is rebelling against the authority of the one who sent him, and is held accountable for the results. Minister, do you wish to have a clear conscience? Then proclaim the fullness of the message, even when you know men will be offended thereby. Who would you rather offend, sinful men, or the holy God?

The warning to men of God to be on guard for themselves and for the flock is couched within a sober reminder of the supernatural nature of the Christian ministry. Paul says the Holy Spirit made them overseers, yet, as we have already seen, Paul ordained elders and instructed Timothy and Titus to do the same thing. The fact that the

Spirit uses means to express His purpose is here exemplified, as is the spiritual nature of the calling to ministry. The very Holy Spirit of God is ultimately the One who prepares and calls men to ministry. This is why the ministry can never be treated as just another vocation, and its success cannot be determined by human standards.

Having made reference to the high calling of the gospel work, Paul is quick to ground his comments in real-world warnings. He does not predict that difficult times would come; he *knows* they will come because he knows the nature of fallen men. His political incorrectness is Spirit-borne: those who disturb the peace of the church and draw disciples away after themselves are not just men with "a different view" as we are told today; they are "savage wolves." They are not content to stay outside the fellowship. They come in "among you," within the fellowship of the church. In fact, they will arise from within the eldership of the church itself. Men with whom we thought we shared close fellowship can disappoint us deeply, hurt us deeply, as they veer off into heresy and purposefully seek to take as many of the sheep with them as they can. They speak "perverse things," though, to the disaffected member and the religious hypocrite, the words they speak sound wonderfully attractive, fresh, and new. This is where deep hurt can come to the faithful minister who has worked long and hard at consistently preaching the word, only to see those he thought were sheep hungrily devouring the perverse words of falsehood, though they *should* know better. They draw the sheep after *them*. They are looking for personal followers, personal religious authority over others. They want to produce disciples who will look to them for guidance.

Paul knew this hurt. He names specific men who had once been in the fellowship of the church but who had left for any number of reasons, including the love of this world. He tells the elders they must remain alert, vigilant, and watchful. He had included sober warnings in his teaching about the difficulties that accompany ministry and the danger of false teachers. Just as he had warned them, so too they must now put that warning into practice and pass the same attitude of care and vigilance on to the next generation of leaders.

As he closes his admonition, Paul commends these men to the only things the church needs to fulfill the Lord's will for her throughout her earthly sojourn: God and the word of His grace. He does not direct the church to external sources, popes, prophets, councils, or upcoming revelation. She is directed to God and the word of His grace, and that alone. God safeguards His people. The word of His grace fills her ears and gives Spirit-borne guidance. Oh, that each generation would be content with God and the word of His grace!

> **Romans 10:8** But what does it say? "THE WORD IS NEAR YOU, IN YOUR MOUTH AND IN YOUR HEART "-- that is, the word of faith which we are preaching,

The Apostles preached "the word of faith," the message calling for faith in Jesus Christ and acceptance of the promises of God toward all who would repent and believe. So constant was the centrality of the call to faith in Christ that Paul does not say "which we preach occasionally" but instead identifies it with the act of preaching itself. Preaching that does not call us to faith and direct people to Christ is not genuine Christian preaching. This thought continues a few verses later:

> **Romans 10:14** How then will they call on Him in whom they have not believed? How will they believe in Him whom they have not heard? And how will they hear without a preacher?

Preaching is ordained of God as the means by which the promises of God in Christ are communicated. When we command men to repent and believe, both terms assume a certain level of knowledge on the part of those repenting (from what?) and believing (in what or whom?). Preaching is the means by which that knowledge is communicated. Could God bypass human agency? God has all power, so surely He could. However, He has chosen to use us and bless us in the process. Anything that removes the scandal of the message preached (both repentance and self-denying belief in Christ as Lord and Savior are offensive things) cannot be called by the high name "Christian preaching."

So much more could be said on a positive level concerning the nature of Christian preaching. Its content is always centered upon the message of the cross; it is always God-honoring; it eschews the wisdom of the world. With these major pillars established, we turn now to examples of pulpit crimes, seeking not to provide any kind of exhaustive list, but instead giving representative samples and categories. These will allow the reader to examine a wider range of preaching and hopefully see whether or not the Word is being honored in the proclamation. As man bends his mind to find newer and even more egregious ways of committing pulpit crimes, it is my hope that these foundational inquiries will provide a solid basis that will be useful in the difficult times ahead. My desire is not to discourage, but to encourage men of God to remain faithful to their calling, and to find in their ministry great joy in serving the King of kings who sees, hears, and observes every moment of preparation, every moment of prayer, and every word spoken in His name from behind the sacred desk.

# CHAPTER FOUR

## The Rap Sheet

The days when the ministry was looked upon with respect and admiration in Western culture are, of course, long gone. There was a day when the minister was elevated to a place of respect, and for good reason. He was seen as a leader in the community, the voice of morality and goodness, a fountain of wisdom. He was there when we were born, there when we were married, there when we were sick, and there when we died. His was an indispensable role in society.

Those were the days when you could openly speak about God, faith, and the Christian life. Now you are only to speak openly about how good homosexuality is, how we should do whatever is good in our own eyes, how each has the right to choose for himself, and how Christianity is responsible for a major portion of the world's woes. Only the doctor is there at your birth, marriage is now optional if not backwards (and no longer just between a man and a woman), your HMO is there when you are sick, and your lawyer when you die (a necessary evil). The minister's field of knowledge and wisdom has been greatly diminished, and it is now limited solely to an area of agnostic speculation anyway. All religious opinions are equal to one another. No one really knows, and, in fact, religion is just a matter of choice anyway, unlike science, which is the new orthodoxy.

Even if the ministry had remained as disciplined and focused as it once was in major parts of Western culture, its position in society would have changed a good bit anyway. Of course, many would say the fall of the ministry is more the ministry's fault than it is anything else. The self-disciplined, personally humble, focused, and dedicated minister may still be out there, but he is the victim of multiplied scandals over many decades. Just as a used car salesman may well be honest, it is his profession, and the proliferation of charlatans in that profession, that reflects on him most strongly. As Western society has sought to marginalize God, it has become its joy to watch ministers fall. The media loves nothing better than a scandal in religion, for then the "religious hypocrisy" card can be played with impunity. Nothing sells better on the front page of the tabloid either. The tortured conscience loves to remind itself that "the church is full of hypocrites." It quiets that voice...for a small while.

But just as damaging as scandals and failures on the part of orthodox, professing ministers, is the tremendous growth of false teaching and unorthodoxy that has been the death knell to the role of the ministry in our culture. As the spectrum of religious belief has exploded over the past decades, and as media has allowed an ever-expanding audience for every kind of cult and ism, the range of what the world sees as "Christian ministry" has become mind-numbingly diverse. While some can tell the difference between the obvious huckster selling his snake-oil religion, many others either cannot, or will not. Everyone, the orthodox and faithful, the heretic, and the huckster—all get thrown into a single vat and stirred together into the thick soup called the Christian ministry.

## The Impact on the Pulpit

The authority that was once invested in the pulpit as the place where God's will was made known (not only for individuals but for the nation as a whole) wasted away in the collective conscience of most Western societies as more and more authority was transferred to secular sources and to the individual. What this has meant for the preaching ministry cannot be underestimated. Not only does the world view the pulpit with suspicion, or even humor, but the church has very much lost a sense of the holy and the authoritative in the pulpit as well. As the church's confidence in the reality of God's voice being with His people through His Word has been shaken by attacks from the realm of science (Darwinism, psychology, destructive literary and historical criticism), so too has the pulpit diminished in its place in the life of the church as a whole. Those who fill the pulpit are hired and fired with sufficient regularity so as to preclude the congregation from viewing the ministry as anything more than a temporary service anyway. This only adds to the problem.

At the same time, the view of the source of the minister's authoritative proclamation, the Bible as the word of God, has suffered a precipitous decline in the large portion of academia, including places of religious education and instruction. Many who stand behind the pulpits question the inspiration and consistency of the Bible, and, no matter what kind of spin you put on it, once you are uncertain about the Bible, you will not inspire confidence on the part of your hearers. As one of my church history professors said in seminary, "What is a mist in the pulpit is a fog in the pew." A lack of deep-seated conviction and confidence in the pastor's heart will result in even less conviction and confidence in the hearts of the congregation. Many a minister has been crippled in his proclamation by succumbing to the, "Many good men have disagreed about these things, therefore..." syndrome. Surely, the wider the spectrum of teachings that are expressed in the culture the more difficult it is for God's voice to be heard with clarity (such is the nature of God's judgment upon a land), and this diminishment in confidence in whether the Bible is sufficient for our needs has greatly impacted the rise in pulpit crimes. Something has to rush into the vacuum created by the loss of the word of God as the central aspect of preaching.

The reasons for the current state of the church in the West are many, and we have touched on just a few of the main issues. While great benefit can be obtained by looking at how each of these movements began and how they were promulgated in the church, such inquiries lie far beyond the scope of this survey. Instead, for now, we need to put together a rap sheet, a quick listing of the kinds of pulpit crimes prevalent in our day.

## Prostitution

The first pulpit crime that comes to mind for most is one known throughout history, going even before the inception of the Christian ministry into the history of the people of Israel via the priesthood. Prostitution normally involves the selling of one's body, but in this case we are speaking of the selling of that which only the pulpit can provide: authority over the people of God. The minister whose motivation moves from heartfelt loyalty to God's truth and love for the people of God to the fading, passing things of the world is selling his own soul.

Money is a root of all kinds of evil, and the carnage it has wreaked behind the pulpits of Christian churches over the centuries cannot possibly be imagined. The repeated warnings of Scripture about the allure of the things of the world and the need for transparent honesty on the part of those in the pulpit in this area of life are there for a reason. While scandals used to be the big problem in this area, now the real perversity is shown in the open: unashamed teaching that it is God's will that Christians be rich and possess the things of the world. The "name it and claim it" heresy is one of the greatest pulpit crimes of the modern era, and it is a sure sign of judgment upon our culture.

### Pandering to Pluralism

Christianity makes a claim that by definition forces it to stand apart from the rest of man's religions. If, in fact, God has entered into His own creation uniquely in the person of Jesus Christ, then He, and He alone, is the only way by which one may come into the presence of God. This claim is highly offensive to modern men. They are quick to attack the claims of Christianity and to call upon Christians to abandon the claim that Christ is the unique Son of God and the only way of salvation.

When those behind the pulpit capitulate on the very nature and definition of the faith, the resultant anemic Christianity is a sad, even disgusting, thing to observe. When the ambassadors of Christ are willing to present Him as one way amongst many, the cross is denied, the gospel rejected.

### Cowardice Under Fire

The hatred of the world for the gospel is strong, and it is consistent. Every believer has felt the sting of rebuke and rejection upon speaking about God's law, man's sin, and God's way of salvation in Christ. Many can confess that, at times, they have shown cowardice under fire and have flinched from doing the right thing (confessing the faith, speaking the truth) because of the fear of the faces of men.

Those who are entrusted with the ministry of the word from the pulpit are especially the objects of the fire of the enemies of God. There is a reason why the Scriptures use illustrations drawn from warfare and the military to constantly exhort us to "stand firm." The man in the pulpit is to be a model in refusing to compromise when under the attack of the enemies of God, for when he runs in the face of the enemy, the sheep are left without protection and guidance.

## Entertainment Without a License

The pulpit is a sacred place where God meets with His people, instructs them, and gives them guidance as they worshipfully gather to hear His truth. To replace that high and divine purpose with the worldly and the commercial is high treason. The church is to be united in its desire to worship God in spirit and in truth. God is not honored when the pulpit becomes a place of entertainment, where His word is replaced with antics intended to placate unbelievers and attract the curious. Yet this is exactly what we see in the largest portion of the church today: entertainment has replaced worship, amusement has replaced the sober contemplation of God and His ways. This is a pulpit crime of immense proportions.

## Felonious Eisegesis

The pulpit is the place where God's word is to be proclaimed. To show proper honor to the One who has given His word, the text of sacred Scripture must be handled with great care, great discipline, and loving diligence. When the Bible is mishandled and sloppily proclaimed, men's ideas take the place of God's truth. Reading into the text ideas and concepts that would have been foreign to the original writers and far beyond their intention is called *eisegesis* rather than the appropriate activity of *exegesis*. One activity gags God's voice, and the other honors Him and edifies the saints. In far too many pulpits today, discipline has been overthrown in the name of some kind of "the Spirit will give me the meaning on the fly" concept that leads to some of the most incredible misrepresentations of Scriptural truth. Few pulpit crimes are as damaging in the long run, and yet this one is so rarely rebuked.

Closely related to felonious eisegesis is the replacement of divine truth with human tradition in the proclamation from the pulpit. Though the Reformation saw a great recovery of truths long encrusted with layer upon layer of unbiblical tradition, as movements progress, they inevitably create their own sets of tradition. It is the constant task of each generation to sort through these traditions, keeping what is in harmony with the word of God and useful in elucidating and protecting that truth, and getting rid of that which fails the test of Scripture. Often, we will confuse our tradition with the word of God, equating the two, and the results can be disastrous, especially when men begin to defend their traditions with a zeal that should be reserved only for divine truths. Just as eisegesis twists and distorts God's message, trafficking in tradition simply dresses man's thoughts and ideas up in divine clothes and sets them before the people for their adoration and obedience. Just as the child of God cannot long bear with the mishandling of God's word, so too that soul will find tradition unsatisfying.

## Cross Dressing

Few issues have generated as much literature over the past decades than that of the role of women in ministry, particularly in reference to the question of whether it is biblical and God-honoring for a woman to stand behind the pulpit and authoritatively instruct the people of God as an elder of the congregation. From that ultimate question, numerous others have arisen relating to teaching, church government, social constructs, and, ultimately, to the hermeneutic we will use to interpret God's will for the church today. Can, or more importantly, should a woman have a position of authoritatively proclaiming God's will to the entirety of God's flock? Clearly, if a church or denomination does not believe the Word is to function as the norm for answering such questions, the answers given will be significantly more varied. However, for those who do believe the Word sufficient to express God's will, the answer to the question seems straightforward.

There surely is no question, however, that some of the leading heretical teachers in the post-evangelical world today are women, and they have garnered a wide and influential following.

## Pulpit Fiction

What happens when the person behind the pulpit becomes fully convinced that he, or she, is absolutely central to what God is doing in the world, and everyone else needs to listen to what they have to say? What happens to the church that grows massive under the leadership of a single individual? What happens after all the millions of books are sold? Who can hold a super-star preacher accountable to the Word? And if that person begins to go off course, heading into error and even heresy, can anyone stop him? We have seen the results of allowing personality cults to develop in the church. Often those who receive great adoration and praise become "stars" and lose their way, falling off into all sorts of pulpit crimes, and, in the worst situations, becoming purveyors of false gospels. Since they have "credibility capital" from building a large church or in some other fashion gaining popularity, people follow them, to their own destruction. They parlay their former authority into a means of selling pulpit fiction instead.

**Body Count**

Mega churches--they are the fastest growing churches in America. If you want to be on the cover of *Time*, visit with Larry King, and have the spotlight, you need members, baptisms, and a sanctuary the size of a shopping mall. These are the keys to being truly "successful" in the ministry, are they not? That is what we are told, for surely, size means God is blessing! Besides, anyone who wants to be able to pay off their student loans from seminary needs to keep "moving up the ladder" to be able to afford those payments.

Of course, those who have been through the "mega church" experience can tell you that most churches that advertise 20,000 members can rarely find 7,000 who are regular in their attendance, and only half that number are regulars in Bible Study. And only a thousand are involved in any kind of meaningful fashion in actually doing something in the church. In some of the new breed of mega churches, they've done away with membership completely, and you get the feeling you are entering a big, wide-open theater with a Sunday (or Saturday night) performance going on, though you only see a few folks with any regularity at all. The idea that this is a cohesive body where things like holiness or church discipline are practiced is foreign to the entire project. This is mass entertainment, mass "evangelism."

What is the result of pressing for numbers, numbers, numbers? Can it be done without sacrificing the very heart of worship? What if God actually wanted a *small* church in a specific location? Could He find a man who would be filled with joy in pastoring such a group?

What kinds of pulpit crimes have resulted from just trying to increase the numbers you send into your denominational headquarters at the end of the church year? How high can we get the body count?

## Identity Theft

Baptism and the Lord's Supper--two divinely-instituted ordinances of Christ's church, established directly by His authority, given to the church for a purpose. Both identify us and mark us out as unashamed followers of Christ. Baptism is a sign of our union with Christ, and the Supper is a means by which every believer proclaims the Lord's death until He comes. The ordinances identify us, and join us together in a common bond, a common confession.

However, for those churches that have become places of non-committed entertainment, the ordinances are a "take it, leave it" concept. If you want to do that kind of thing, OK, but if not, we won't press the issue. The idea that these are divine institutions, demonstrating the very wisdom of God, vital for the health and growth of the church, is not consistent with the "get them in the door and entertain them" methodology that is all the rage today. By short-selling these divinely-given gifts that connect us to one another, many in the pulpit are committing identity theft.

## Warranty Fraud

There is a particularly widespread and pernicious pulpit crime that is very much theological in nature that should be noted and warned against. It is a form of teaching that is deeply entrenched in many conservative churches, primarily in the American South. It is a form of easy-believism (a soteriological heresy, if we are truthful) that denies entire swaths of God's revelation concerning His purpose in saving a people "zealous for good deeds." It is a teaching that says that one is saved solely and merely by entertaining, even if only for a moment, a particular set of beliefs about Christ (and even then, it is a very shallow, short list of facts about who Jesus was, and little more). After this initial act of "faith" a person is "saved" and that is all there is to it. That person never has to be concerned about holiness of life, never has to express love for Christ or faith in God's word, and can go out and become an atheist, Buddhist, Muslim, or Mormon; it matters not.

His or her "ticket is punched," and there is nothing else to say. Salvation is sure, even if there is never a scintilla of Christ-likeness produced in their lives. This kind of teaching is not just imbalanced; the Bible identifies it as false and deceptive, and, since it leads many to a false assurance, it is a pulpit crime on the felonious level.

## Where Are the Cops?

Finally, given all the pulpit crime going on in the church today, what can be done about it? Where are the cops? Is there anyone we can turn to? Well, of course, obviously, there is One we can turn to, and we must turn to Him in humility to seek His mercy and grace in the recovering of a biblically balanced and non-worldly view of the preaching ministry. We do not need to seek some kind of external authority to step in and "set things right." Christ still reigns over His church, and He will do what is right in His time and in His way. We are to pray, to serve, to remain faithful, and support wholeheartedly those men who consistently discharge their duties.

There are surely many specialized works (primarily in journals of pastoral study and practice) that address each of these pulpit crimes in depth. This work is meant to spur thought and wake up the reader to the issues that are presented to us by the inspired word of God. The ministry of the pulpit is much maligned, and in general, ignored today, but it is my hope that this work will cause the reader to consider well the importance the pulpit has in Christ's rulership of His Church.

# CHAPTER FIVE

## Prostitution

**2 Corinthians 2:17** For we are not like many, peddling the word of God, but as from sincerity, but as from God, we speak in Christ in the sight of God.

Sincerity in handling the word of God---this is the mark of the man of God who walks in the manner the apostles walked. Yet, even in their day, not just a few, but "many" walked another path. They peddled the word of God. They sold it for profit, traded it in, and, by extension, adulterated it and corrupted it, all for the sake of base personal gain. Paul had seen it, as had all the other apostles. Even in their day, men dared use God's truth to line their pockets. Oh, surely they would have denied the charge. Some would have complained about how unloving and judgmental the apostle was to cast aspersions upon the ministry of others, all the while protesting the purity of their motivations. But Paul knew better. He knew there were those who would gladly sell the very truth of God for whatever they could get for it. Such have no fear of God, and they do not realize that the true minister "speaks in Christ in the sight of God." Those who are not in Christ cannot speak from that vantage point, and hence they care nothing for the sincerity that marked the Apostles' respectful handling of God's truth. But for the believer who has been called into ministry, nothing could be more reassuring, more exciting, more comforting, or more supportive than realizing that when we handle God's truth before God's people, we do so "in Christ in the sight of God." Truly He comprises an audience of

One, and He is the only audience that really matters. Of course, God knows the motives of the heart of every man who stands behind the pulpit, and He judges on that infallible basis.

Few things have corrupted men in the ministry more than the temptations that arise from handling money. While the ministry is often associated with poverty, for that very reason ministers are often entrusted with serious funds, and are expected to handle them aright, always putting godly interests first. Even the most non-religious person knows the minister is supposed to be free from the love of money, so any indication that a minister is hypocritical in the matter is received with joy by the enemies of the faith. In our day, scandals regarding money are reported with glee by the media, and even the flimsiest of evidence is taken as a validated, verified fact, as long as it impugns the character of a "Bible believer."

Fulfilling the biblical teaching that there is nothing new under the sun, the Scriptures contain warnings that are directly relevant to us today regarding the selling of the precious privilege of the pulpit for that which is passing away, the things of this world. When giving Timothy guidance regarding the qualifications for the eldership, Paul taught:

> An overseer, then, must be above reproach, the husband of one wife, temperate, prudent, respectable, hospitable, able to teach,  3 not addicted to wine or pugnacious, but gentle, peaceable, free from the love of money. (1 Timothy 3:2-3)

The final qualification is not that he be poor. It is not that he lack any and all business sense, or have some kind of martyr complex. It is the *love* of money that is in view. This seems to have been a component of Paul's teaching, since he would later use the phrase in a similar fashion, one that suggests Timothy was quite familiar with it:

> For the love of money is a root of all sorts of evil, and some by longing for it have wandered away from the faith and pierced themselves with many griefs. (1 Timothy 6:10)

It is not money that is the problem. Money is used by God every day to provide for His people and accomplish good. But it is the *love* of the *means* of this blessing that Paul warns about. Some people love what they can do with money; others simply love money for the power they think it gives them. A person with money becomes a little god, shaping and making his own reality, his own future, or so he thinks. It is that kind of love of money that is a root (not *the* root, as the KJV puts it) of all sorts of evil. The sins the love of money can engender are many, even in the context of the church. Dishonesty, perversion of justice and truth, showing partiality---all can be traced directly to an improper love of money, which itself is a manifestation of a rejection of God's will and purpose in our lives, a refusal to be content with what God has given to us. While this is vitally important for leaders, in this they only mirror the truth that all believers are called to this, for, as the writer to the Hebrews said, "Make sure that your character is free from the love of money, being content with what you have." (13:5) How can we be content in a world that is constantly seeking to make us discontent? The same text tells us: we have God's promise that He will never desert us, He will never forsake us. He is our treasure, He is our portion, and, if we delight in Him, we have all we need. As the hymn writer well said, "Turn your eyes upon Jesus, look full in His wonderful face, and the things of earth will grow strangely dim, in the light of His glory and grace." What commands our hearts will determine our desires, and if the hearts of God's ministers are filled with joy at their task, there will be no place for the love of the things of the world, including money.

## Heretical Money Grubbing

As badly as the church has been hurt by scandals related to the dishonest handling of money, it has taken a black eye because of the prevalence of the "Word-Faith" teachers. They teach it is God's will for you to be a lover of money. In fact, all you have to do is name it and claim it, and it will be yours. Whether you are claiming money ("seed faith giving"), possessions, health, success—whatever pleases your little heart, God will give at your command, very much like a genie in a bottle. All you need is "faith," whatever on earth that is (since it has little resemblance to the biblical term). While being afflicted with such false teachers would be bad enough, the fact that the confessing church has been so slow and quiet to denounce this perversion of Christ's gospel is almost as damaging!

There is no end to the eisegetical gymnastics these heretics will use to promote their beliefs and line their pockets. Any text is liable to be twisted into the service of the teacher, man or woman, seeking to get the gullible to pick up the phone and drag out the credit card. I have sought to be as general as possible in this work and hence have avoided names so as to not distract the reader, but in this case I may well describe a particular false teacher so clearly her identity will be known. I will never forget sitting down one evening when I was fending for myself, in the absence of my family, with a meal from the drive-through window down the street. I flipped on the tiny television in the kitchen and, as I literally turned the dial to find a station (the TV is that old, and is black and white!), I ran into a woman preaching on a nation-wide "Christian" television network. I say "Christian" in quotes because this particular organization gives a voice to just about every heretic who has the money to buy airtime. Once in a while, I will watch this network just to remind myself of what things are like "out there." So, I began listening to this woman. She's a pleasant looking lady, at least, but she can talk about three times faster than I can, and that is saying a lot. I'm not sure she was actually breathing during this rant, and that is the only way to describe what I was listening to, a rant. She speaks in a staccato fashion, keeping your attention if for no other reason than you wonder how anyone can talk that fast without spitting. If I recall correctly, she was "preaching" from a single text in Psalm 63, and, somehow, had come to the conclusion that this text meant that those in the audience, if they really believed God, would be picking up their phones to demonstrate their faith by giving $63 to her ministry. Well, of course, they could show a lot more faith by giving twice that, or three times that, or ten times that, but they had to start with $63 because the text she was peddling and perverting and distorting was in Psalm 63. She was standing before a group of folks who were loudly amening her, at least when she actually stopped long enough for them to get a shout in edge-wise, and behind her a whole group of "worshippers" were waving their hands and stomping their feet and "praising God." I caught myself sitting at the counter in my kitchen with a little corn-on-the-cob in one hand, staring at the tiny television, not only shocked, but utterly disgusted as well. "One thing is for certain," I said to myself and anyone else close enough to hear me, "whatever religion that woman is promoting, it has nothing, absolutely nothing, to do with mine."

Those who live luxuriously on the lack of discernment of so-called Christians provide defenses of their beliefs, of course. But every single one of their defenses share one thing in common: an incapacity to bear close examination in light of *all* of Scripture. It is easy to latch onto a promise here, a proverb there, a statement there, and in so doing build a theology about how the sons of God are supposed to live like kings in this life. However, as the simplest Christian reading his Bible knows, there is a good deal of material about suffering, difficulty, persecution, crucifying our sinful desires, mortifying the flesh, and all sorts of other things that put the lie to these false teachers' house of cards.

I have always found it shocking that the kind of teaching that denies the place of suffering in the lives of God's people and that promises health and wealth and physical prosperity carries an attraction outside of the decadent West. I see these false teachers flying their personal jets into third world countries and filling sports stadiums with poor people who, I can only imagine, are hoping for some kind of miracle in their quest for a better life. It is truly a crime of immense proportions that these men and women will fly back out of these poor countries with more money than they had when they arrived. One would think that eventually the word would get out, "This stuff doesn't work," but like the lottery (rightly called a tax on the mathematically challenged), people keep trying in hopes of "getting lucky." And in the process the gospel of Christ is trodden in the mud yet again. Someone will have much to answer for in the judgment.

### Is Love of Money the Only Evil?

While the love of money is a powerful agent in drawing men away from the truth, there are related dangers that need to be kept in mind. Religious power can be just as addicting as monetary gain, and there are those who are willing to trade finances for authority and control over others. They will often make a show of their poverty but at the same time enslave people to their authority and control. This kind of abuse is rampant in religious cults and isms, and sadly, tens of thousands today labor in the chains of religious deception in tiny little cults barely known to any outside of a small circle.

However, there is a more subtle form of this kind of temptation that is truly rampant. I refer to the many times each Lord's Day when parts of God's truth get trimmed, muted, or obscured, all because of a desire not to "lose" the support of an individual or group within the fellowship of the church. This is often the case within the context of those ministries that are placed under the "church growth" pressure of particularly large denominations. The reasoning is simple enough: without the support of group X or donor Y in the congregation, there will never be enough funding to accomplish project Z. Project Z is the only way the denominational leadership will be convinced that our church is truly growing and progressing in the proper way. But group X or donor Y do not like doctrines P, and E, and even though the minister sees that preaching through the next passage of Scripture in, say, Romans, will raise the issue of doctrines P and E, he is immediately faced with a dilemma. Honestly handling the text will offend group X and donor Y. He is convinced that project Z is part of "God's will" for the church. So what must be done? The answers are varied, but they all involve "spinning" the text. It may require just skipping the offending texts, or reading them but never actually commenting on them. Or it may involve just a little bit of misdirection, reading the text but then immediately heading for the hills, topically speaking, and never really getting back to what those verses actually say, hoping that no one will notice because they were so impressed with the detour and the sleight of hand.     A few heart-tugging stories definitely help in accomplishing the task. Or you may just need to pull out the faithful and trusty eisegesis tool and come up with a satisfying (for group X and donor Y, anyway) way around the actual meaning. Would a minister ever actually do this? Sadly, the answer is "yes," and that with a frequency that should sadden every godly heart.

Let's say our hypothetical minister safely navigates the treacherous waters of Romans and makes it through with group X happy, donor Y giving, and project Z completed. Is there really anything wrong with the result? Have the ends justified the means? Before answering, realize that many would look at project Z and say, "See, this will help us to reach more people for Jesus! That is all that matters!" That kind of argument carries tremendous emotional weight with many today, and it is hard to argue against "results." But truly, as we have already noted, "What you win them with is what you win them to." What does it really mean to "win them to Jesus" when you are actually afraid to speak Jesus' truth to the gathered body lest some become offended and leave? What kind of community *of faith* is this anyway? Jesus said His sheep will hear His voice (John 10:27) so do we think ourselves wise enough to know when to muffle the voice of the Savior found in His Scriptures? Do the ends actually justify the means, and do we have the right ends in mind anyway? How is God glorified when we decide it is better to take another route to our self-designed concept of "success"?

Over the past two decades I have had the opportunity and privilege of teaching theology and apologetics in a seminary setting, and I have seen the effects of putting unbiblical (and hence ungodly) pressure upon young men to live up to some standard of "success" that is the creation of the minds of men and nothing more. I have seen their spirits crushed by the awful load of trying to live up to charts and graphs in their churches. Is it any wonder that they reach out hungrily to almost every passing fad and program? They are not allowed to grow and mature along with their people. They are not allowed to fall in love with the Scriptures nor are they encouraged to preach the Bible in its entirety. Instead they are given not-so-subtle instructions to avoid certain "divisive" topics, avoid the "complicated stuff" (when was the last time you heard a moving, exegetical, passionate sermon on the Trinity?), and just basically try to "keep people happy" while not "driving off the seekers." The idea that the gospel *must* offend those who remain in rebellion against Christ seems to have missed the architects of this kind of church growth strategy.

Who loses in all this? God's glory, the gospel, the church as a whole, the minister personally, and the true sheep of God. That's a wide swath. God is not glorified when His ministers decide which parts of His truth are appropriate and which parts are not. The gospel cannot be chopped up into bits and pieces with the parts that offend the natural man taken out. That is no longer a gospel that saves, for the natural man *must be offended* for God uses that offense to bring him to his knees before the cross and the throne. The church is damaged for it ends up filled with driftwood, with rebellious religious hypocrites who have salved their consciences enough to hang around but have not been convicted enough to be converted. The minister personally suffers, for God never blesses the editing of His truth. The first time he intentionally "fudges" on a text he may feel a strong twinge of guilt, but the second time it gets easier, and before long he is utterly numb to the entire idea of rightly handling the text to God's glory. And the true sheep of God unfortunate enough to be in that ministry are left feeding on husks, empty shells of the truth, pious platitudes without application, vague truths without teeth or power. The cost is high for such "success stories," to be sure.

So we see that prostitution of the pulpit can take many forms, and the heart trained in godly wisdom can start from this point and see many more applications than the few we have brought out. Once again we see the importance of having an "audience of One," that is, keeping as our singular goal the glorification of the One who has called us to the ministry, gifted us, and placed His Word within our hearts and souls and minds so that we cannot know any greater joy than its study and proclamation. As long as we are looking around at others we will never have the singular focus that will allow us to persevere through the greatest trials, especially when those trials do not arise from without, but from within, the church itself.

# CHAPTER SIX

## Pandering to Pluralism

Inclusive. Open. Accepting. Welcoming. Aren't these the watchwords of our society today? Isn't that what everyone wants to be? These are attractive, warm words, are they not? Compare words like exclusive, judging, narrow, confined. These are cold, harsh words. No one wants to be described as narrow or judging or exclusive. These are "buzzwords" of modern Western thinking. Whether they are actually being applied in a meaningful or logical fashion is a completely different issue, and for some, even asking the question proves you are anything but open and accepting and welcoming and, well, let's face it, loving!

It is the "loving" challenge that many find difficult to overcome today. If our society says it is "loving" to say Jesus is *my* way but not necessarily the *only* way of salvation, and we know Christians are to be loving, then what is the problem? What is lost by allowing that there might be some other way for others, while presenting a passionate plea that you find Jesus the best way? The allure of the position cannot be denied, and this explains how it has become so widespread. Add to this the fact that so few churches/denominations have a solid foundation in an inspired, inerrant revelation from God upon which to build a case for an exclusive claim on the part of Christ (if it is all just one writer's opinion and there is no consistent revelation contained therein, who can trust it to have final authority?) and you have the perfect environment in which to breed an entire generation of "I like Jesus, He's fine with me, try Him out, you might like Him too" inclusivists.

A wonderful example of this is found in the comments made at the Washington National Cathedral on Easter, 2005, by George F. Regas, Rector Emeritus, All Saints Church, Pasadena, California. Note the heart and soul of a true pluralist:

> My hope this morning as your preacher is to bring us all into a closer identity with the inclusive spirit of Jesus.
>
> Christianity is often presented in the most exclusionary ways. In today's Gospel, John puts words on Jesus' lips that have led Christians through the centuries to claim an exclusive way to salvation. "I am the way and the truth and the life. No one comes to the Father except through me." That is one of the most difficult verses in the Bible to interpret adequately. Those who claim that Christianity is the exclusive way to a saving faith cling tenaciously to this verse.
>
> Jesus said, "I am the way, and the truth and the life. No one comes to the Father (to God) except through me." If my reflections on this verse are to have integrity, I must speak as though my close rabbi friends and my Muslim colleagues are sitting right there in a pew in front of me. Those good people in whom I've seen the glory of God.
>
> I can no longer think about Jesus as the only way to God and to a saving faith. How one comes into a relationship with God has taken on a meaning that it did not have in my younger years. "I am the way, and the truth and the life. No one comes to God except through me." The first thing I want you to explore with me is this: I simply refuse to hold the doctrine that there is no access to God except through Jesus.
>
> I personally reject the claim that Christianity has the truth and all other religions are in error. Unfortunately, this is the position of the new Pope, Benedict XVI, who says salvation is only possible through Jesus Christ. I think it is a mistaken view to say Christianity is superior to Hinduism, Buddhism, Islam, and Judaism and that Christ is the only way to God and salvation.
>
> Although the majority of American Christians probably believe that salvation is possible only through faith in Jesus Christ, I find this to be a profound distortion of what Jesus was about in his ministry.
>
> My reading of the Bible points me to a God whose love is inclusive and universal. This thought is very significant because it was this proclamation of universal love that got Jesus into trouble. The flags of exclusivism were flying all around Jesus, and he

steadfastly resisted each one of these seductive invitations to belong to us only and exclude the rest. Jesus loved them all. He put his arms around everybody—and they killed him.

Consider well what this self-professing Christian minister said on that Easter Sunday in one of the most famous churches in America. Jesus' words in John 14:6 are clear, straightforward, and in the context of the Gospel of John, rather simple to understand. Rev. Regas' problem is not that the words are difficult "to interpret adequately," it is that they are difficult to explain away. They do not fit his worldview, hence, they are "difficult." He clearly, at one point, shared the Christian view that God had become man definitively in Jesus Christ so that He is the only way to the Father, but now he has experienced things in his life that have led him to reject this teaching. They seem to be "personal" things, for he says he has seen the glory of God in his Jewish and Muslim friends. Because of this, he "refuses" to hold to the doctrine that Jesus is the only way to the Father, and he rejects the idea that Christianity is true while other religions are false. Notice he does not explain Jesus' words, he just refuses to accept what they mean. He claims the historic understanding of the teaching of the entire New Testament is a "profound distortion," but he does not explain how or why. Rev. Regas claims, "My reading of the Bible points me to a God whose love is inclusive and universal," but one is forced to conclude that this "reading" is highly selective—it must ignore entire swaths of biblical history, let alone the mountains of questions raised by God's very specific acts of judgment in the past. That reading likewise must involve the removal of all texts about God's holiness, wrath against sin, atonement, judgment, and the like. A bit more honest statement would be, "My rejection of Christian belief has led me to selectively reinterpret the Bible," for that is truly what is in view here.

These high-profile defections from the faith in the name of a "gentler, kinder Christianity" are tremendously common today, but they need to be seen for what they are. Rev. Regas expressed it well. "I simply refuse to hold the doctrine that there is no access to God except through Jesus." He did not say, "I have been convinced by Scripture." Regas is not standing with Luther before the Emperor at Worms appealing to Scripture and reason. He is rejecting Scripture, plain and simple. The foundation of faith in

God's revealed truth crumbled long ago in Regas' denomination, and truly no one can expect someone who does not stand with the Apostles in believing "it is written" to believe in the radical claims of Christianity! Without a sure word from the Lord, the claims of Christ are incomprehensible and highly offensive. For those who wish, for sentimental or traditional reasons, to retain the name "Christian" while jettisoning all the accompanying definitions and substance, pluralism is a soft landing spot, a nice, warm, sentimental alternative that is as harmless (and meaningless) as a fuzzball. But let's be blunt and clear: such a Christianity has nothing at all to do with the faith for which the martyrs have died, and to call that kind of humanistic philosophy "Christianity" is to engage in historic and biblical dishonesty.

### Ashamed of the Gospel

The kind of open rejection of central aspects of Christian teaching contained in the preceding citation is common in much of what continues to call itself Christianity today. But all who wish to honor God's Word must state clearly that anyone who says Jesus is *a* way of salvation and not *the* way of salvation is not preaching the gospel of Christ and is not trusting in that gospel, either. Jesus is not *a* Savior, He is *the* Savior, and that is not a "negotiable" belief.

The Christian faith proclaims that there is but one true God. He is the creator of all things, and He has created purposefully. He is sovereign over human affairs, and He is directing all things to His own glory. Already this basic, foundational platform has excluded major portions of today's professing Christianity, but the biblical support of these basic assertions is overwhelming. Only a wholesale rejection of the Bible's authority can lead one to any other conclusion.

This sovereign God has revealed His law to His creatures, who, in their representative head, Adam, have fallen into sin and rebellion, bringing death and decay into God's creation. God has chosen to demonstrate the full spectrum of His attributes in how He brings glory out of man's fall, redeeming some by uniting them to Jesus Christ, and demonstrating His wrath and power and justice in bringing judgment upon others. This He does freely and solely upon the basis of His own will.

The decisive action God has taken in accomplishing His purpose is the incarnation of Jesus Christ. The eternal Son entered into human existence as Jesus of Nazareth. This was a *unique* event. God has not come many times, but once, definitively, finally, at a particular point in time, in Christ. He is the God-man, fully God and fully man, and by His singular atoning work in voluntarily giving Himself on the cross of Calvary, He has borne the wrath and punishment due to the elect in Himself. By God's mercy and grace alone they are saved, all to the praise of God's glorious grace.

God the Father has testified to the truthfulness of His Son's claims by raising Him from the dead and seating Him on His right hand. The resurrection is not only God's seal upon the ministry and claims of Christ, but it is His promise that those who believe in Christ will, like Him, conquer death and experience eternal life.

Now, this brief overview of the outline of Christian theology, though passing over a number of important sub-topics, is sufficient to explain why all forms of pluralism are incompatible with Christian profession. To put it simply, Christianity's claims are simply too *big* to fit in such a scheme! If God's purpose involved the coming of Christ *from the very start*, then the idea that He would be just *one of many ways* is incoherent. Further, the fact that redemption must be provided by God (not merely *a way* of redemption, but *redemption itself*) closes the door upon "other ways" for they do not meet the standard: they cannot satisfy God's justice. Further, if there are other ways of redemption, then the sacrifice of Christ becomes a mockery, an empty charade without meaning, and the Father is convicted of gross cruelty to His own Son.

The entirety of Christian theology militates against pluralism. Throughout the Bible the focus is upon what God has done to reveal Himself, not through men's religions, but through the law and the prophets, pointing to their fulfillment in Christ. Christianity cannot play nicely with other religions, because to do so is to cease being Christianity. Christians actually have the audacity to claim that Jesus Christ was uniquely the God-man, the Creator of all things, the Judge of all the earth, and that the eternal destiny of every single human being will be determined by their relationship to Him. God chose to glorify Himself in this fashion and no other, and to claim the right to overturn His purposes is, at best, arrogant on the part of the creature, man.

The impulse to pluralism is fully understandable. As long as there are many religions of equal value with one another, man, the creator of these religions, has "control." No one can really say, one way or the other, and it is all left in the realm of opinion and taste. Besides, if you don't like what one is offering, you can go "shopping" for something better. Just as pagan religions would often acknowledge other deities and even work out syncretistic forms of cooperation, so too modern man's religions continue the trend, all the while uniting against the one true enemy. In history, monotheism was considered the opponent of all the religions of Rome, for example. The Jews were hated for denying the existence of other "gods," and the Christians were even called "atheists" for taking the same stance. The pagan nations around ancient Israel hated them for their exclusivity and were always seeking to cause compromise through the worship of multiple deities. And so it is today. When Christianity stands firm in its proclamation of one God who has revealed Himself decisively in Jesus Christ, it is hated by the world, including the world of religion. When "Christians" are willing to abandon the central claim that Jesus Christ is the *one* way to the Father, *those* religious people will be adored by the world and promoted as living examples of what it means to be "loving Christians."

It might be good at this point to clarify the difference between pluralism proper and another term often used in this discussion, inclusivism. Pluralism allows for the co-existence and equality of differing religions, as seen in the citation above. Jews, Muslims, Hindus, Buddhists, and Christians, all get to have "true" religions, equal with the other, all leading to God. Inclusivism, as it has become popular today, is the cheap man's Christianity. What I mean by that is that it tries to get the warm fuzzies guaranteed by pluralism without giving up the obvious centrality of Christ inherent in the Christian faith. But it does so by sleight of hand. Realizing that there is no way to pretend fidelity to the Christian scriptures while adopting open pluralism, inclusivists have bent their mind to finding a way around the exclusivity of faith in Christ. So, they have redefined what it means to believe in Christ. They have removed knowledge of Christ from the equation so that any heartfelt religious impulse is reinterpreted to be equivalent to having faith in Christ. That way, the "honest Buddhist" who bows before his idol is actually showing faith in Christ, though he doesn't know it. The Muslim who throws stones at the devil in Mecca is actually showing faith in Christ, despite actually denying Christ's death and resurrection. All "faith moves" toward God are faith moves toward Christ, so that He will save those who act in this kind of "faith" in spite of their ignorance.

Inclusivism challenges the orthodox believer not because it has more biblical basis (it doesn't), but simply because it redefines the terms of the argument and moves the target, all at the same time. Those who do not start with a sound theology find it very hard to respond to this kind of argument. First, the mere assertion of a position is not the same as providing a biblical foundation for it, and inclusivists struggle mightily to come up with any kind of positive evidence for their case from Scripture. The Bible is clear that faith has an object, and it is not God's purpose that those He draws to Christ remain in ignorance of Him. Since it is His will to conform His people to the image of Christ, it is mighty odd that He would do so without them having a clue who Christ is in the first place. And how strange that the early Christians suffered so much for their confession of faith in Christ when the Apostles never intended that anyone should have to suffer for confessing His name! They could have simply "gone with the religious flow" and kept a secret "faith" in their heart and all would have been well. As the reader can see, one must start with a very defective, man-centered concept of the gospel to be able to reason to the point of inclusivism.

**The Battle Lines Are Drawn**

Where does the child of God find eternal life? In Christ. Forgiveness? In Christ? Adoption into the family of God? Only one place. In Christ. What is the over-arching call on our lives? Growing in the grace and knowledge of our Lord Jesus Christ. To whose image are we to be conformed? Jesus Christ. Has God given testimony of any other by raising him from the dead? He has not. Has God given multiple, contradictory revelations of His holy nature and His law? He has not. Has God told one people He is pleased with one kind of worship, but another a completely different kind of worship? Surely not. Pluralism requires us to abandon the most basic forms of logic and adopt a view of God that makes Him as irrational and self-contradictory as the mass of man's religions. Christians cannot do this, for they believe God has created this world, and He calls us to worship Him in truth. He has to have revealed the *way* in an understandable and consistent manner.

The reality of what is being demanded of Christian believers in Western society today must be carefully considered. The pressure to adopt a pluralistic/inclusivistic stance is strong throughout the length and breadth of Western cultures. So it needs to be understood that when we are asked to give equality of *weight and value* to all religious perspectives, we are at the same time being asked to *deny fundamental elements of Christian belief.* Jesus Christ cannot be *unique* in the ways He Himself claimed, the world tells us. He cannot *really* be the Creator, He cannot *really* have risen from the dead, He cannot *really* be returning again, He cannot *really* be the Judge of all the earth. You can believe those things *but only in a partial fashion.* You cannot cross the line and actually believe that anyone else must see Him in these categories or you will be violating the fundamental dogmatic orthodoxy of Western culture, that there are no certainties outside of what can be seen and felt and measured in the natural realm. What the culture demands is nothing less than capitulation on the Lordship and deity of Christ, and that is a compromise no born again child of God can make. Where does your ultimate allegiance lie? With Christ, the King, or with the cultural elite who refuse His Lordship? Are we ashamed of the Gospel, and more so, the One who gave Himself for us?

## Let's Be Loving

One more quick admonishment for believers is necessary here. We would experience much more joy in our Christian lives and especially in our witness if we would on a daily basis remind ourselves that the term "love" is defined by God in His word, not by the culture in the newspapers and other media. "Don't be so unloving!" is the battle cry of the pluralists and the rest of those in our culture who oppose the kingship of Christ over His creation. But who gets to define what "loving" means? For a Christian, love begins with God. He defines it, and our love for Him must be supreme, conditioning and ordering all other loves. And just how *loving* is it for rebel sinners to tell God what He can and cannot do, how He will be worshipped, and just how far He can go in demanding of us our service and loyalty? Is it really "loving" to allow our fellow creatures to continue in their deception and false religiosity when all it will do is bring them to the judgment seat of

God without hope and without forgiveness? Is it loving to allow the clear, clarion call of Scripture to be mocked and derided by men while we sit idly by, paralyzed by fear of "offending" someone's sensibilities? Who are we showing true love for when we allow the gospel of grace to be corrupted into a mere suggestion, the cross turned into a massive cosmic mistake, and the empty tomb into a novelty of uncertainty? We need a clear, often repeated reminder of what *Christian* love involves, and first and foremost it directs us to the Triune God and to fidelity to His truth and His gospel. Let us love God boldly in the face of the enemy, for He may well use our love as a means of bringing more of His own into the family of faith!

# CHAPTER SEVEN

## Cowardice Under Fire

World War II General George S. Patton detested cowards. In a famous incident that eventually cost him further advancement, Patton slapped a soldier who had shown less than exemplary bravery in the face of fire from the enemy. He refused to allow those who were injured in anything less than a way he felt appropriate to be treated in the hospital along with the "real" soldiers. Patton's "blood-and-guts" mentality helped win the war in Europe and made him a hero in the eyes of many of those who served under his command. But Patton was a pagan, a foul-mouthed sinner, and the loyalty he inspired was based upon a common hatred of the enemy, not upon the quality of his person or character. And like all men, he left this world to face his maker and judge.

As unpopular as it is, the Christian faith has always used military language in its self-descriptions. From the Psalms the warrior king David would speak of being surrounded by enemies, of flying arrows, of hands trained to war. In the New Testament the Lord Jesus Himself spoke of kings going to war and likened Himself to just such a royal commander and ruler. The Apostle Paul pressed many military examples into service, likening himself to a soldier who needed to wear particular kinds of armor to accomplish the duties assigned to him by his master. He called upon all believers to "fight the good fight," to resist the adversary, to wield the sword of the Spirit. Throughout Scripture the Christian life is likened to warfare, with a goal, and resistance in reaching that goal, and an enemy of our very souls who must be studied, and resisted, with God's help.

Of course, the sphere of the warfare of the New Testament is spiritual, not physical. The power of the church is not found in allegiance with governments or military forces, but in the only power given to her, the very power of God in the gospel. The church has a "weapon" that can actually change the hearts and minds of men, and it is a weapon that, when used by a sovereign God in accordance with His purposes, is unstoppable in its power to bring about God's glory and the salvation of His elect people.

The call of God's word to bring the message of Christ's lordship to a world that loves its sin and rebellion does indeed bring us into conflict with those of the world. It was not without reason that the Lord Jesus said:

> "If the world hates you, you know that it has hated Me before *it hated* you. 19 If you were of the world, the world would love its own; but because you are not of the world, but I chose you out of the world, because of this the world hates you. 20 Remember the word that I said to you, 'A slave is not greater than his master.' If they persecuted Me, they will also persecute you; if they kept My word, they will keep yours also." (John 15:18-20)

Persecution. Hatred. It does not sound like the Lord was predicting a quiet, peaceful relationship between His disciples and the world. There would be conflict, warfare, struggle. Internally, yes, warfare with the world and the desires of our flesh. And externally as well, for as we live our lives under the lordship of Christ, our very walk— the fact that we refuse to think like the world, adopt its ways, its language, its dress—acts as an irritant, a convicting proclamation that Christ's kingdom is *still* here and simply will not go away! Sometimes that battle can become deadly violent as martyrs face the hatred of communism, or Islam, today.

In Western cultures the opposition we currently face takes less violent forms. The media in particular loves to attack the Christian faith and anyone who would hold firmly to its claims, often brandishing the "unloving, narrow-minded fundamentalist" bat in an effort to bring about compliance. Christians face discrimination in the workplace if they hold to their convictions and refuse to "go with the flow." More than one qualified believer has been passed over because their superiors did not want "Holy Joe" ruining their fun. And the educational institutions of our nations have become very hostile ground for any person unwilling to offer a pinch of incense upon the altar of the academy. There in the hallowed halls of education the truly religious nature of naturalistic materialism is seen in all its glory, and the Christian who would remain faithful to Christ will of necessity have to commit many acts of heresy by violating the dogmas of the academy. Often, punishment and retribution are swift.

In light of all these things, it is perfectly natural that many a believer struggles with the desire to retreat from the battle, especially when the conflict reaches a fever pitch. Those with retiring natures can find it very difficult to follow the apostolic command to "Be on the alert, stand firm in the faith, act like men, be strong" (1 Cor. 16:13). Even the naturally strong and resilient can be beaten down by the constant barrage of messages from the culture to be silent, to be ashamed of Christ and the claims we make for Him. The world knows how to make us pay for fidelity to the truth. Every believer can fall into the trap—slowly, imperceptibly at first—of learning to "flinch" when the time comes to stand firm in the face of the world's denials of Christ's lordship. To what do I refer? We can pick up the habit of avoiding situations where we know we might be faced with challenges or opportunities of witness. When topics like homosexuality, abortion, ethics or morality arise, we find an excuse to go elsewhere, or we change the topic. Or we learn to "spin" our replies so that we can at least internally believe we spoke the truth while at the same time avoiding the confrontation that radical commitment to Christ inevitably brings with the rebellious world around us.

Compromise is seen the most clearly when it is found in the pulpit. When the proclamation of Christ's kingly rights over His creatures is watered down so that the minister can avoid paying the price, externally and internally, for speaking the truth, God's honor suffers. External costs can include the opposition of the community, including other churches and organizations, even to the point of protest (as evangelical churches have discovered in the face of radical homosexuals). And in those churches where the dividing line between the world and the church is precariously thin, and the thinking of the world has flooded through the doors and filled the pews with worldlings wearing only a thin veneer of religiosity over their rebellion, the cost to the minister to remain firm even in the face of fire from the fellowship itself can be even greater.

The Western media is quite adept at focusing the pressure to compromise on those who would find themselves standing before their cameras or sitting in their television studios. Recently a well-known post-evangelical leader, who pastors a massive church and has written a few books that have been mega-best sellers, appeared on a nationally syndicated talk program with a well-known interviewer. This particular interviewer is adept at phrasing questions to Christians in the most pointed, and often unfair, manner. He directly and asked this pastor about the exclusive claims of Christ. He asked him, "What about Jews and Muslims?" He was exemplifying the common approach of the world to the issue of Christ being the only way of salvation. The pastor faltered. Instead of explaining that all people, no matter what their "religion," have broken God's law and abide under His wrath, and hence must have a perfect and sure way of forgiveness, and that this way is found only in Jesus Christ, the Incarnate One whose death *alone* can redeem and who *alone* has risen from the dead, the pastor balked at knowing who would and would not go to heaven. When asked directly if acceptance of Christ was necessary, the pastor said only God could judge the heart, which, while that may be true, is hardly relevant to the point. He then spoke of traveling to non-Christian nations and how he could tell those of a completely different religious faith "loved God" and were "sincere." To this he added that he wanted to have a relationship with Jesus, which, sadly, in the context, made it sound like having a relationship with Jesus is a matter of taste, but not a matter of salvation. To his credit, the pastor apologized a few weeks later for his all-too-public collapse, but the damage was done, for the apology could never have the scope, or the power, that a firm, unflinching testimony would have had when the opportunity was presented.

Thankfully, others have not failed when the cameras were turned on, but despite their faithfulness Western culture gladly covers its ears and closes its eyes to their testimony. The fact remains that the enemies of the cross *rejoice* when the servants of Christ turn tail and run in the heat of battle. They hate the claims Christ makes on their lives, so when they can force someone who confesses His name to compromise, to spin, to waver, they are encouraged in their rebellion. We must remember that the Scriptures teach that men *know* God exists and are actively involved in suppressing that knowledge (Romans 1:18-21). It is not easy to invest so much energy in holding down the voice of conscience, quieting that image of God and its repeated testimony that you are a rebel and you know the day of judgment is coming. So it is easy to understand why unregenerate men and women become angry with those who have given up the battle and surrendered to their Creator and Lord. Each faithful Christian is an everyday reminder to the unregenerate of their own rebellion and sin. Since God is outside the realm in which they can be active in causing harm, His representatives bear the brunt of their annoyance, or their anger.

**Removing God's Wrath**

There is no question that the Scriptures speak often, and clearly, of the wrath of God. No one can seriously argue that God's wrath is merely extraneous to the Bible's depiction of God, His law, sacrifice, atonement, or justification. His is a holy wrath, a wrath aimed at those who love rebellion and sin, and it is a wrath that has broken out in judgment in the past, providing an example to curb evil in the present. And though room precludes a fuller discussion of the subject, the love of God is only seen in its proper revealed balance when it is seen as a gracious love, and that can only be seen against the backdrop of God's wrath. Most of the errors that have arisen regarding the nature of the cross work of Christ can be traced back to a defective understanding of God's wrath and man's sin. If you do not see the wrath of God in the cross, you are not fully seeing His love there, either.

But Western culture thinks it has "grown up" and no longer wants or needs a God of wrath. In its limitless wisdom it has cheapened God's love by removing from God full personhood. He is no longer angered at sin, no longer concerned about His law, but is more than vaguely like that bearded old man of pagan lore, sitting benignly upon His throne, clumsily trying to set things right in a world truly out of His control. Those theologians more concerned about friendship with the world than fidelity to Christ have quickly abandoned the biblical testimony to God's true nature and have allied themselves with the world in seeking to create an "acceptable" portrait of God, one that will not trouble sinners by reminding them of His just standards and law.

The collapse into liberalism and the consistent hatred of the world have resulted in a diminishment of balanced, biblical preaching on the subject of God's wrath. While a few might be tempted to overcompensate in the other direction, becoming the stereotypical "hellfire and damnation" preacher, in the majority of cases the pressure from the battlefront does not bring about a direct denial of the unpopular belief, but instead a simple lack of focus upon it. Ministers know what will bring them the accolades of their people, and they know what will bring them stony silence and disapproving stares as well. Only odd people like being rejected and disliked, so, the long-term impact will be to turn the preaching away from those topics that are unpopular, controversial, or while known to be true, are rejected openly by society. So once again we return to a consideration that is central to our discussion: for whom do we preach? Where is our loyalty, our heartfelt desire to please? Do we view ourselves as ambassadors, delivering even the unpopular portions of our Master's message, or do we think we have the right to edit the message as we see fit given our "cultural context?" The answer to this question will determine whether we flee the battle or stand firm.

### Hiding Behind the Pulpit

One clear example of how cultural pressure can result in fear and intimidation and retreat in the proclamation of the gospel is found today in the topic of sexual morality, and especially, abortion. We will discuss the particular issue of homosexuality later under the topic of twisting the Scriptures, since an entire movement has arisen claiming one can practice homosexuality as a Christian and they have sought to support this position from the text of Scripture. But when it comes to such issues as sexual morality and the murder of unborn children (if that phraseology bothers you, you have already succumbed to the culture's attack upon your sensibilities and thinking), we find ourselves in a field where biblical morality and ethics speak very loudly, but so many behind pulpits today cower because of the fear of rejection and hatred that comes from speaking the truth.

The abortion issue illustrates how far Western society has declined in its own self-contradiction and self-hatred. There is no real question about the humanity of the unborn child from a scientific viewpoint. The more we learn about the developing child the more obvious it is that a unique individual is in view that, unless violently killed with poison or scalpel, will develop and become a self-sustaining, unique human being. But Western society detests children and family, and is only concerned about self-improvement, not about legacy, tradition, the betterment of others. Hoard it all, let everyone else fight over what's left, seems to be the idea. So all the evidence that we are in fact murdering innocents right and left and in the *vast* majority of cases for nothing but the sake of convenience and financial well-being, is irrelevant as long as the society places no value upon human life to begin with. Together with the denial of man's unique nature as a creation of God, this devaluing of humanity is having far-reaching consequences.

The Christian faith speaks clearly and forcefully to the underlying issues in the abortion debate. Yet, how many ministers today flinch, if not in the pulpit, at least in the office, when it comes to the high calling of sexual purity? How many treat marriage not as the high calling it is in Scripture but instead seek to reflect worldly values? From every angle a biblically literate Christian has this issue covered. From the angle of God's sovereignty, of God being the creator of life (making life precious), of God determining the roles of men and women and how they are to relate, and of what is best for the human family, calling us to deny selfishness and to serve others---the Christian faith can address the entire spectrum of issues surrounding abortion.

Yet, as anyone knows, there is no single, clarion voice of Christianity on this topic. Abortion advocates hail from almost every sector of what calls itself Christianity. In entire denominations that a century ago stood firm on moral and ethical values, the god of humanism has been set up in the holy of holies, and as a result, the heartless murder of unborn children is proclaimed a Christian virtue from behind the pulpits of those churches and denominations. What a tragedy! Those groups that have sought this kind of "cease-fire" with the society in hopes of being "attractive" have only attracted unbelievers at the cost of the gospel itself. The world is not impressed by compromisers and those who flee in retreat from the frontlines of battle. They know who is still standing strong and who is not, and while they may laud the compromisers while in the spotlight, in their private moments they know who is who.

Martin Luther once commented:

If I profess with the loudest voice and clearest exposition every portion of the truth of God except precisely that little point which the world and the devil are at that moment attacking, I am not confessing Christ, however boldly I may be professing Christ. Where the battle rages, there the loyalty of the soldier is proved, and to be steady on all the battlefield besides, is mere flight and disgrace if he flinches at that point. (Luther's Works. Weimar Edition. Briefwechsel [Correspondence], vol. 3, pp. 81f.)

This is a truthful observation, one needing to be heard in every generation. Profession of Christ, and confession of Christ, are different things, and this reality has been lost to most today. You can speak the words, but if you are unwilling to live in their light when the enemy attacks, your profession is empty. Confession goes beyond words to actions. The enemy knows that if he can "take the hill" of the pulpit he has destroyed the divinely-ordained means of communication, and has won the battle. We see the wreckage of many a church strewn across the landscape, solemn evidence of the reality of the battle that is raging, whether observed by the world or not. Will we rally round the pulpits of those faithful strongholds that are left, constantly praying for those who minister there, supporting them, encouraging them? It is to this that we are called.

# CHAPTER EIGHT

## Entertainment Without a License

Even before the service begins, you can feel the excitement. Music is playing in the background, and people are milling about. They are obviously looking forward to what is about to take place. Soon a praise band begins to take their places on the professionally lighted stage. The video screens, which have been scrolling pretty pictures along with announcements of a wide variety of ministries throughout the week, switch over to the words of the first praise chorus. The driving beat immediately has everyone on their feet as the professionally performed music fills the room. People in jeans, shorts, Hawaiian shirts, mesh into a jumble of upstretched arms and swaying bodies. Each chorus is met with applause. The music raises the emotions of the audience, and then transitions them into a more "worshipful" attitude, causing some to weep.

After twenty minutes the audience is seated and a "special music" number sets the mood for the "time in the Word." After the soloist demonstrates her vocal talents to the applause of the gathered crowd, the minister approaches the...music stand, as there is no pulpit to clutter the perfectly lighted and balanced stage. The lights are set up to accent his very hip clothing, khaki pants and comfortable shirt. The sermon/talk/sermonette/counseling session is perfectly designed to flow with the musical themes already established. Particular words and phrases, once regular in evangelical church services, are conspicuous by their absence, though no one seems to notice. All are assured of God's love and His ultimate desire that they experience His plan for their lives. Heartwarming stories are told, and the talk ends on an emotional high note, long before anyone could possibly become tired or bored. The musicians almost magically appear as soon as the last word of the prayer is uttered, and the entire service ends as professionally as it began.

Sound familiar? If you have attended the fastest growing churches in the post-evangelical landscape of Western culture, you've seen variants of it over and over again. Sometimes you throw in some drama, maybe a multi-media presentation, a mime show. Even more entertaining versions are being played out for the kids in another well-designed room down the hall. After the service is over, everyone can go relax in the coffee bar/snack shack out in the foyer.

Now before the howls of protest begin, let me say that I do not necessarily find every item I just included in my description sinful or a "pulpit crime." For me and my community the majority of the above format would not fit into what we consider to be the proper attitude of worship, no question. But I am not the legalist one might think, as I believe the elders of each local congregation have the ultimate responsibility before God to determine, within the context of God's revealed will concerning His worship, how they are going to discern with a heart of wisdom the best way for their congregation in their setting to fulfill the Lord's commands for them. I do not believe a tie and jacket for the preacher, for example, is demanded by Scripture in every culture and at every time. I do believe, however, that everyone's dress should reflect their coming into the presence of God Himself, and if a person would feel odd meeting the President of the United States dressed in a particular fashion, they might consider what that means when going to enter into the presence of God with fellow believers. But, the issue has to do with the overall purpose and concern of the entirety of the worship experience, and how each of these elements is related to the other in accomplishing that purpose. Who is at the center of all of this? Is it the worshipper? The lost person coming in from outside? Or God Himself?

A number of years ago I was speaking at a conference in the Chicago area. A very professional, talented "praise band" would sing before each session (and then, I noted, promptly leave). Right before I was to speak on the Roman Catholic dogmatic teachings concerning Mary, they took to the stage and the lead singer said, "Before we finish our time of worship and the speaker comes, let's stand and sing together." I was immediately struck by the statement, and when I took the podium to make my presentation, I began by stating that I did not believe that the worship had just ended, and that in fact, it was continuing in the proclamation of God's truth via the spoken word. I do not believe the performers heard my statements, as they had already left to go perform somewhere else.

What is the purpose of the gathering of the body of believers? We saw in our earlier study what is to take the center of the gathering of believers. We discerned from the New Testament accounts, and in particular from the pastoral epistles, that the singing of Psalms, hymns, and spiritual songs was part of corporate worship. Communal confession of the faith, the ordinances (baptism, the Lord's Supper), prayer, the reading of the Scriptures, and preaching (exhortation/preaching/correction/encouragement) are all elements of worship. I definitely do not find anything telling us in what order these must be done, or that you can't have "praise teams" or anything of the like. But one thing does seem to stand out: outside of the fact that the exhortation comes from those entrusted with the task, all of these activities are *communal*. That is, they do not exalt or point to individuals. Instead, the community comes together to worship. The worship involves singing, prayer, the reading of Scripture, and the exhortation to sound doctrine and godly living. These are all part of worship, and they all point away from self and the earthly and lead us to the contemplation of the divine.

There is something else to see in these elements of Christian worship. I would argue, given the nature of New Testament teaching, that the reading and preaching of Scripture is the central act in the list provided above. Why? Because the gifting of the Spirit to which Paul refers is focused upon that very area, i.e., teaching, discernment, and it is through that medium that correction, exhortation and training in righteousness, takes place. It would also be the time when the saints would be gathered and hence that kind of instruction would take center place, whereas one can always sing Psalms and hymns and spiritual songs (though not all are gifted at it!) even when alone. In any case, the gathering of believers for worship involved a communal confession of faith, prayer, and Scripturally-based proclamation and instruction.

What is missing, of course, is entertainment. None of these things are intended to make the saints "happy," and one thing is for sure, none of these things are meant to attract the lost by appealing to their desire for amusement and entertainment. And the real question is, should we "spin" these divine activities so that they *are* attractive to the lost? And what of those in the congregation who have become apathetic about their faith? Should we make sure the prayers are so bland they will not bring conviction? The preaching so vague and general and "feel good" that no one will be offended? Or is it not painfully obvious that it is just this method that God has given to us to be used by His Spirit in bringing conviction to the hearts of God's people, and healing to their lives?

It is highly doubtful the pagans that surrounded Israel found His worship at the Tabernacle or later in the Temple in Jerusalem "entertaining." I suppose there are synagogues today that have gone for the entertainment appeal, but I do not get the feeling that this was normative in the days of Paul and the apostles. The early church likewise, persecuted, racked by controversy and false teaching, was hardly a place of ease, comfort, and entertainment.

Nor would it be a place where the unbeliever could find solace, a salve for a hurting conscience not leading to repentance. There was no easy-believism in a day when you would lose your life at the end of a rusty Roman sword for confessing the faith. The church was deadly serious, so the farthest thing from the minds of the primitive Christians was attracting folks with a show and a message of self-affirmation. There were no praise bands when you had to sneak out in the woods even to sing, and even then, you did so at great personal and corporate risk.

The entertainment form of "worship" could not have existed in the days of the Apostles. It requires an established church structure and a social setting that allows for the creation of a culturally conditioned form of Christianity. Only when an argument can be made that "worship" is mostly concerned with what the *worshippers* experience and "feel" can an entire theology of worship centered on something other than God develop. Persecution, suffering, deprivation—all these things purify the church of self-centeredness and worldly ambition, so it is during those times when the church is suffering that her worship is often the most pure. When she is blessed and prosperous in the world's goods (making one question the use of the term 'blessed' to begin with) then she can turn her eyes earthward and begin to satisfy her desires of self-fulfillment.

There is another major factor that gives rise to entertainment in the place of worship: man-centered theology and a man-centered gospel. If you do not trust the power of the Spirit and word to bring men and women to repentance and faith, but instead think that the final arbiter of whether God will succeed in the gospel or not is in fact the rebel man, you will use just about anything at your disposal to bring about that ultimate "good" of a person "accepting Jesus." So if you are willing to manipulate their emotions, tug at their heart strings, and in general wring a "decision" out of them through such means, you will likewise try to get them in with any kind of attraction that will work. Put on a show, try to look like the theater down the street, put on a raffle, sell lottery tickets. As long as it works, right? Keep them coming back long enough and who knows, they might just sign on the dotted line, and won't Jesus be lucky to have them on His side!

The problem is, once you get them "in" with that mind-set, guess what? You get to keep them in the same way! For some odd reason, folks entertained into the kingdom expect the amusement park to remain open. In fact, they have the nasty propensity to ask, "What have you done for me lately?" That is, if it was a show that got them "sorta quasi-religious," well, you better be careful. Your show might become boring, and there is always a new show down the street, ready to bring them, and their never-really-sacrificial donations, in for a front-row seat. And thus the church-hopping culture develops, those poor lost souls who move from church to church, entertainment source to entertainment source, convinced they are right with God, the "almost Christian" as one writer has put it, yet as lost and undone as can be. You cannot entertain folks enough to save their souls. At some point the truth has to be spoken with clarity. We are not saved by osmosis. The gospel calls us to a decisive break with the old life, a turning away, an embracing of the new.

**Let God be God**

To this point I have not focused upon the egregious examples that abound today of gross, crass entertainment. Clowns serving the Lord's Supper or the most indiscreet "liturgical dance" are well known abuses that very few seriously attempt to defend. The church that raffled off a Hummer just recently likewise is probably not quite up to mounting an exegetically satisfying defense of such commercialism. For the large portion of those with any sense of biblical propriety and balance, these kinds of things are obvious abuses. So what is troubling is to find churches that confess the inspiration and supernatural character of God's Word and yet, in spite of that, they do not show any abiding trust in its promises regarding how the church is to function and how it is to grow. And so they are willing to grab hold of worldly means to attract rebels, all the while corrupting (a strong, but perfectly valid term) the worship of God through the introduction of all sorts of activities that are not conducive to the propagation of truth and are not helpful to the people of God—all because they are not commanded or allowed by the Spirit in the divine Scriptures, the only place we are to go to know what is pleasing to God in His worship.

As we have seen, there are two primary areas of concern when it comes to entertainment in the church: entertainment as a means of winning or attracting the lost, and entertainment as (at best) an aid to worship or, at worst, a replacement of it. The second problem is often associated with a false view of church growth. The first risks the purity of the gospel, the second the purity of God's worship and the health of the church. Both are closely connected because they demonstrate the wholesale invasion of the church by the world, and they illustrate together the truth that what you win them with is indeed what you win them to. It is next to impossible to use defective means of evangelism and then turn around and call for sound biblical Christian experience.

Reformed theology has always spoken of what is called the "regulative principle of worship." Entire books have been written on the subject, and I risk offending my Reformed brethren by simplifying too much here, but I will take the risk anyway. In a nutshell, God gets to determine what is pleasing to Him in the matter of worship. That just isn't our decision, it is not our choice. Of course, Reformed folks differ with each other over the specifics of how to work out the "regulative principle" (normally abbreviated RPW) in every detail, but one thing is for certain, the result of being concerned to worship God not according to the dictates of my conscience or in the light of my feelings but in light of His revealed will produces a much more narrow spectrum of practice than anything else.

I will never forget the first time I attended the church where I now serve as an elder. I had never heard of a "Reformed Baptist" before, and was, at the time, part of a large, conservative, evangelical church. When I came into the service on a Sunday evening, I immediately noticed how quiet it was in comparison to what I was used to. There was no effort to get the congregation excited prior to the service. In fact, I saw people...praying! Some were reading their Bibles. As the elders came in there was a sense of reverence and anticipation. The service was simple, straightforward, much like the surroundings. Hymns, prayer, the reading of the Scriptures (from the Old Testament no less!), and very quickly the sermon began. The preacher (now my fellow elder, having served the same congregation for over three decades now) was working through, of all books, *Amos*. As a soon-to-be graduating seminary student, I was most impressed. Anyone who can preach through Amos is a brave and hearty soul. But the sermon was pointed, applicatory, and challenging. I will never forget the impression made upon me that evening, for I knew I was among people who took this to be an opportunity of worshipping God by obediently hearing His word. I was changed by that realization.

My tradition is looked upon by many today as backward and slated for extinction, and, if the future belongs to those who adapt Christianity to the culture, they may well be right. But I dare suggest that the true church has been built by Christ in His way, in His time, for many generations, and that would seem to indicate that He will continue that process as long as He chooses to do so. That means people will keep looking to the word as their guide and will discover this concept of humbly accepting the Lord's revelation as to what is pleasing in His sight, the centrality of the proclamation of His word in worship, the importance of exhortation to godliness, warnings against sin, exaltation of Christ's perfect work—all important aspects of true God-honoring Christian worship. God may allow His people to live through times of great confusion and even massive apostasy, but He will continue to build His church, and His Spirit will guide His people so as to fulfill the Scriptures, "to Him *be* the glory in the church and in Christ Jesus to all generations forever and ever". (Eph. 3:21)

The real issue in the scenario with which I began is this: why? Why do we do what we do? What is our ultimate goal? Why do we dress as we dress? Why do we allot time as we do in our services?

Why do we preach as we preach? Why do we sing, and why do we sing it the way we do? Do we care about what the world will think of our activities? Where is God in all of this? Do we seek to meet Him in His truth, begging the Spirit to use the word to reveal to us the depths of our own hearts so that we may be changed and made better servants of His? Do we think He is lucky to have us around, or do we tremble at the thought of approaching Him, not out of fear of retribution or wrath (being in Christ), but because we stand in awe of His glory, His power, His condescension, His grace? Are we more concerned about making a misstep in our performance for the audience, or about the purity of the motives of our hearts before the God with whom we have to do? These are the questions that separate worship from entertainment.

# CHAPTER NINE

## Felonious Eisegesis

It was another one of those odd moments when, like a kid suddenly overtaken with the urge to swipe that piece of candy, I turned the dial on my little television to that channel I never mention, and the "Christian" television network broadcast thereon. Evidently hunger causes my level of discernment or discipline to waver. In any case, as I was preparing a quick dinner I listened to an African-American preacher speaking to a *huge* crowd. He was speaking from 1 John 3:2 in the KJV, "Beloved, now are we the sons of God, and it doth not yet appear what we shall be: but we know that, when he shall appear, we shall be like him; for we shall see him as he is." For some reason, men were standing all around the platform, and it was quite noisy as he moved from side to side behind the pulpit. I tried to follow his comments as best I could, but there did not seem to be any particular connection between his thoughts. And then he caught my attention when he started talking about the translation of the verse. Those who have taught Greek tend to get all excited about such things. I stopped working on my food and once again found myself staring at the little screen as I listened to this man. Part of what fascinated me was what he was saying, yes, but also, I was watching the audience accepting and yelling "amen" at his every word, almost his every gesture.

He began commenting on the phrases, "we shall be like him; for we shall see him just as he is." He told them that there was no word for "shall" in the Greek. I immediately put down a nacho chip and focused. No word for "shall"? Of course there is. The verb is future tense in the Greek! But he wasn't done. He kept going. The text talks about us being sons of God (KJV), and so, without "shall" in the text (he did not really explain why the KJV missed the translation, and it did not seem anyone was interested in challenging his statement), it is supposed to mean, "we be like him." Yes, that's what he said. We be like him. That's what it *should* say. Then he went on to make the application that since "we be like him" then we can by faith control our circumstances and experience victory and all the rest of the word-faith drivel that sells like hotcakes in our "don't give me a Christianity that involves suffering or hardship" world.

Eisegesis. The reading into a text, in this case, an ancient text of the Bible, of a meaning that is not supported by the grammar, syntax, lexical meanings, and over-all context, of the original. It is the opposite of exegesis, where you read *out* of the text its original meaning by careful attention to the same things, grammar, syntax, the lexical meanings of the words used by the author (as they were used in his day and in his area), and the over-all context of the document. As common as it is, it *should* be something the Christian minister finds abhorrent, for when you stop and think about it, eisegesis muffles the voice of God. If the text of Scripture is in fact "God-breathed" (2 Tim. 3:16) and if God speaks in the entirety of the Bible (Matt. 22:31) then eisegesis would involve silencing that divine voice and replacing it with the thoughts, intents, and most often, traditions, of the one doing the interpretation. In fact, in my experience, eisegetical mishandling of the inspired text is the single most common source of heresy, division, disunity, and a lack of clarity in the proclamation of the gospel. The man of God is commended when he handles God's truth aright (2 Tim. 2:15), and it should be his highest honor to be privileged to do so. Exegesis, then, apart from being a skill honed over years of practice, is an absolutely necessary means of honoring the Lord a minister claims to serve. For some today, exegesis and all the attendant study that goes into it "robs" one of the "Spirit." The fact is, there is no greater spiritual service the minister can render to the Lord and to the flock entrusted to his care than to allow God's voice to speak with the clarity that only sound exegetical practice can provide.

Eisegesis arises from many sources. Innocently, it arises from ignorance. Men can approach the text of Scripture without sufficient training, without sufficient knowledge, and inevitably come to the wrong conclusions. But simple errors due to ignorance should be diminished, at least among true believers, by consideration of the glory and honor of the text being handled. One would think men would be very, very careful when handling what they confess to be God's holy revelation to man, but, there is often a disconnect between their profession of faith and their practice. In any case, the spectrum of causes of eisegesis moves quickly from the innocent to the culpable. Untaught and unstable men can misuse the text of Scripture (2 Peter 3:16), and that to their own destruction. God's Word is truth, as Jesus said (John 17:17), so twisting it can only be self-destructive to creatures who so desperately need truth.

Personal desires can likewise lead to eisegesis. That is, unless we honor the text properly we will "find" in the text what we *desire* to find. Sadly, the Bible is often used like a magical talisman. Ever heard of someone saying, "So, I was so concerned that I prayed and then I opened my Bible and I put my finger down and what I read answered my question." That's superstition, not exegesis. That is no better than the wild-eyed (and utterly debunked) "Bible Codes" craze of the late 1990s. Doing that kind of thing is the same as rolling dice: if you have two possibilities in mind, and the verse you just happen to point to contains language your mind can connect to one side or another, you interpret that linguistic or conceptual connection as divine guidance, and blame it on the Bible! Nothing could be farther from the truth! It dishonors God's Word and a wise elder would take such a person aside and explain to them that such activities are completely improper for the child of God. Yes, I know, many a popular leader has reported engaging in just such activities, but that does not make it right.

This kind of abuse of the text of Scripture can often be baptized in spirituality even by those speaking from the pulpit. I remember with great clarity just such an example that arose during that period of the ecclesiastical calendar where this particular church was setting its budget for the next year. Sadly, many an example of Scriptural abuse and twisting has appeared during fund-raising cycles, which is doubly odd in light of the fact that there is plenty in Scripture that can be taken in context and with a proper eye to exegesis that addresses our need to sacrificially give to the work of the ministry of the church. In any case, I was listening to a minister at a large church attempting to present the concept that we can "limit" God by our lack of faith in giving to the church. Though this particular preacher always used the New American Standard Bible, for some reason this one evening he switched to the King James Version. The text selected was Psalm 78:41, which in the KJV reads, "Yea, they turned back and tempted God, and limited the Holy One of Israel." The sermon hinged on the phrase, "limited the Holy One of Israel." Much was said about how your actions can keep God from accomplishing His desires, and how we as a church had to believe God so that He could properly work through us. All of this, of course, was so that we would underwrite a multi-million dollar budget in the pledges about to be turned in.

I checked the NASB's rendering of the text, and discovered why there had been a translation change. It reads, "Again and again they tempted God, And pained the Holy One of Israel." Now that just doesn't fit into the needed fund-raising emphasis. The King James simply missed the translation of the verb (upon examination of the Hebrew it was fully understandable why). But here we had not just a passing example of "get your topic, look for a text," we had a very purposeful "get your topic, if your translation doesn't help, use one that will" maneuver. Of course, I am not saying that every single topical sermon is out of bounds; but there is much truth to the observation, "Having read his text, he very quickly departed therefrom, never to return again." Baptizing your personal agenda as a minister with a text here or a text there does not provide the people of God with proper spiritual sustenance. In fact, it provides them with a very poor example, unworthy of the undershepherd.

While writing this very chapter I decided to try a little experiment. I flipped on that channel again, quite purposefully, to see how long it would take to hear eisegesis coming out of my television set. As soon as the screen came to life, I saw a very popular preacher, who, ironically, has been likened to Billy Graham by the highly discerning mainstream media, though he is not, in fact, even a *Trinitarian,* and I knew I had better start counting the seconds fast, because this wasn't going to take long. It took less than 45 seconds for this preacher to tell a giant group of women (do his audiences ever sit down?) that in the story of the Canaanite woman the woman kept worshipping and worshipping and that, as a result, *she put Jesus in her debt due to her worship.* I checked the time and clicked it off, having found my example of eisegesis so quickly I did not have to keep watching to get even more offended at the abuse of the Scriptures at that popular preacher's hand.

Probably the single worst example of this kind of "grab a text, build a mountain" eisegesis made one man a multi-millionaire and just about single-handedly built a publishing house. I refer to the abuse of a passing comment in 1 Chronicles 4:10:

> Now Jabez called on the God of Israel, saying, "Oh that You would bless me indeed and enlarge my border, and that Your hand might be with me, and that You would keep *me* from harm that *it* may not pain me!" And God granted him what he requested.

The fact that such a text could end up on coffee mugs and t-shirts while entire texts about suffering and self-denial and the like remain hidden away from sight in so many churches is a tremendous example of how far post-evangelicalism has fallen from its beginnings.

### Eisegesis as Necessary to One's Theology

It is hardly surprising that cults and isms engage in gross eisegesis, especially when they have other books of "Scripture" that override the Bible as their final authority. A quick run through the writings of men like Joseph Smith Jr., the founder of Mormonism, will provide some incredible examples of scripture twisting. One of my favorites is found in his comments on Revelation 1:6, which read in the King James Version to which he would have been accustomed, "And hath made us kings and priests unto God and his Father; to him *be* glory and dominion for ever and ever. Amen." Smith, once he developed his concept of a plurality of gods (a concept he did not have when the Mormon Church began) began ransacking the Bible looking for support. Of course, being a self-proclaimed "prophet," he also came up with new "Scriptures," including a book called *The Book of Abraham*, which likewise taught his new theology. In any case, many a text suffered at his hand, but in this case he actually found two gods in Revelation 1:6, God, and God's Father, another god.[2] In reality, the better translation is "to His God and Father," as most modern versions read. The underlying Greek indicates that

---

[2] As recorded in *Teachings of the Prophet Joseph Smith* ed. Joseph Fielding Smith (Deseret Book, 1977), p. 370.

both terms are referring to one person, not to two. Smith's prophetic powers did not seem to include actually reading the original languages (though he certainly tried to make that claim as well, even producing his own "inspired" version).

Space precludes more examples of cultic eisegesis, and that is not our goal at any rate, for we are looking primarily at the pulpit within the professing Christian church. But it is within that context that we encounter what would have been identified as a "cultic" movement only a few decades ago, and yet now is considered so mainstream that it has been embraced openly by entire formerly evangelical denominations. If anyone had ever suggested that one could have a "lying Christian" movement, they would have been laughed at. Or a "murdering Christians" movement, or a "coveting Christians" movement, in which people actually claim that they are made liars, murderers, or covetous, and that since this is how God made them, well, then they can "embrace" their "lifestyle" and still love God and embrace the faith.

But, of course, today we have the "Christian homosexual" movement, and it has infected major denominations and a wide swath of the Christian academic field. To attempt to defend its existence this movement has produced shelves full of volumes all seeking to explain, in a myriad of ways, why they can embrace something the Bible plainly identifies as sin. The result is a literal *mountain* of eisegesis. Most of it is terribly shallow. For example, a number of homosexual writers, in attempting to do away with the testimony of Scripture derived from the record of what happened to Sodom and Gomorrah, cite Ezekiel 16:48-49, and cites it as follows: "This was the guilt of your sister Sodom: she and her daughters had pride, surfeit of food and prosperous ease, but did not aid the poor and needy." That is where the citation ends, and the argument moves on. Evidently, many folks do not check the actual text for themselves, for the next verse says, "Thus they were haughty and committed abominations before Me. Therefore I removed them when I saw it." Obviously, the portion these writers cite gives the background that gave rise to the eventual judgment seen in Genesis 18 and 19, the very text under consideration! This is not so much eisegesis as a blatantly dishonest twisting of the text.

But the homosexual lobby has produced huge texts filled with cross-references and in-depth argumentation, so much so that the very volume of the written works has created its own inertia. Mass of material does not equal quality of argumentation, consistency of reasoning, or accuracy of exegesis. In fact, the mass of the material is self-contradictory. But more relevant to our study of pulpit crimes, the eisegesis offered by these authors, some of whom are credentialed scholars, illustrates another vitally important source of error in handling the Scriptures. If you bring a worldview and desire to "find" a particular viewpoint in the Scriptures, you can find amazing ways to isolate any text and create a plausible way around it. There truly is no limitation to the imagination of the heart of man, and when that heart is joined to a mind that has been trained to deal with original languages and theology, but yet is not under the lordship of Christ, the results can be book-length illustrations of just how hard-hearted men can be.

Consider these words from an openly homosexual "bishop" drawing from the biblical testimony to the resurrection of Lazarus and of Christ:

> You'd think I wouldn't have needed reminding. Years ago, my sexuality seemed like an unmovable stone in my way, a burden so huge that it seemed to threaten every thing I held dear. Accepting being gay seemed impossible; affirming and embracing it was beyond comprehension. And then just as surely as Jesus called to his friend Lazarus to "Come out!" of his tomb, Jesus called me to come out of my tomb of guilt and shame, to accept and love that part of me that he ALREADY accepted and loved. If I would only look up and see that that stone had ALREADY been rolled away, I could have a new, more abundant life. That resurrection changed my life. I thought I would never, ever forget.
>
> But I'm human, and I do forget, from time to time, that God has accomplished the most amazing thing in the life, death and resurrection of Jesus Christ. Something cosmic, and yet personal and individual. And God is always calling me back when I encounter stones in my way, reminding me to stop, look up, and see that the stone has already been rolled away, if I will only see what God has accomplished, surrender to it, and be changed and empowered by it.

The idea that there could be a connection between the resurrection of Christ and this man's embracing of a sinful lifestyle is, for the believer, next to impossible to understand. But for those who do not believe in the clarity of the Scriptures or their authority, their desire to hold to their own worldview rather than allowing Scripture to define it for them allows for this kind of abuse of the text and of divine truths. Christ died upon the cross bearing in Himself the punishment for God's broken law, and it is that very law that this man is flouting by means of his homosexuality! This kind of abuse of the text is common place in many major denominations today, and it has become common because the Bible's own power to define for us such things as good and evil, love and hate, right and wrong, has been lost to those religious groups. That is what would allow a "minister" to say these words from a pulpit not long ago:

> On December 2, the Rev. Beth Stroud, lost all her ministerial credentials in Pennsylvania for being a clergyperson who is a lesbian in a committed relationship. Is her very person incompatible with Christianity, or is it that those who are in loving committed relationships cannot be Christians? This certainly makes you wonder just what is compatible with Christianity? Would you like to be excluded from your faith and your profession because you love somebody? Is it exclusion and abuse, or is it love and understanding? Hypocrisy must end so that all these Christians in name only can open their hearts with integrity and honesty, like Beth Stroud has done, in her relationships with her partner and others.[3]

How can one have a "committed relationship" that is by its nature a betrayal of God's will? How can a minister not know that "her very person" abides under the wrath of God *like every single other human being just as Jesus taught?* God Himself defined marriage in the garden, and the Lord Jesus confirmed that creation ordinance, so it is an overt denial of biblical authority to call a lesbian relationship "loving." Loving for whom? Does it show love of God? No. Does it show love of the other person? No, it is selfish. Does it even show love of self? Only in the sense of self-destruction. If this minister wishes to know what is compatible with Christianity, he might well consider the revealed word, for it speaks plainly to the issue. It is sophistry of the highest level to say that a lesbian

---

[3] Rev. Mark Harris, "The Christian Curse," December 5, 2004.

"minister" is being excluded from something because of love. She should have been excluded by simple obedience to the Scriptures to begin with (see our next chapter), but even here, in the context of this sermon, the exclusion is based upon accepting the Bible's authority to define what love actually is. Clearly, this minister does not utilize a biblical definition of love from the start. Acting consistently with God's moral law is not abusive or exclusionary; instead, it is this minister who is abusing the Scriptures and excluding God's truth. How can anyone pretend to use the terms "honesty" and "integrity" while turning Christian truth on its head while standing behind a pulpit built by the sacrifices of men and women who believed the Bible to be God's Word? It is truly hard to imagine.

One of the most common examples of eisegesis spawned by the homosexual movement is offered in response to the citation by believers of the words of Paul in Romans 1, specifically, verses 26-27:

> For this reason God gave them over to degrading passions; for their women exchanged the natural function for that which is unnatural, 27 and in the same way also the men abandoned the natural function of the woman and burned in their desire toward one another, men with men committing indecent acts and receiving in their own persons the due penalty of their error.

I personally encountered the response offered to this text by many homosexual "ministers" today on a radio debate a number of years ago. They go back in the text and follow the progression, speaking of those who did not honor God or give thanks; then they say, "But I honor God and give thanks." They make reference to those who exchanged the glory of God, and they say, "But I haven't done that." They may go past the verses cited above and continue the process, each time saying, "But see, I haven't done these things," and then comes the conclusion, "So, this text is not talking about me, it is talking about someone else."

When I first heard a homosexual minister present this argument it was live on a radio program. My response was swift and it left the man completely silent. I insisted that this kind of reasoning would completely destroy Paul's argument, for no one could possibly argue that a person had to commit every single sin mentioned by Paul in Romans 1 for each and every one of those sins to be itself sinful. Imagine the foolishness of asserting that as long as I love God, I could gossip, or be disobedient to my parents, or be insolent, or even commit murder, but as long as I haven't taken every action leading up to this list, Paul must not have been talking about me! This kind of twisting of the Scriptures, with the intent to in essence gag God so that He cannot address personal sin is itself morally evil, and will bring God's judgment.     There are other "special interest" groups in the broader church today that likewise have to base their entire existence upon the eisegetical misinterpretation of the text of Scripture, and they do not all populate the left side of the spectrum. One of the most infamous purveyors of eisegesis that moves plainly into the realm of Scripture twisting is a well known head of a radio network who has predicted the coming of Christ in the past (and is doing so once again at the time of this writing) and who has declared that all true believers should leave their churches for God will no longer save anyone inside a church.  This individual, while professing a high view of Scripture, denies this in practice by utilizing a unique form of interpretation that has no rules outside of those he makes up as he goes along.  Numerology and symbology mix together in a mind-numbing dance that allows this radio personality to "find" almost anything in any text at all.  Thankfully, despite the breadth of his radio network's coverage, the large portion of God's people can tell when someone has completely abandoned any semblance of a reasonable means of interpreting the Bible.  But some, always looking for something "new," fall for his false teachings. However, this movement is not long for this world, not because of the failure of his coming prediction, or his advanced age, but because it cannot produce meaningful second-generation leadership.  It is purely a personality cult.  Once the leader is gone, these movements fracture and splinter into a thousand pieces, because, obviously, everyone else is now free to use the same incoherent form of interpretation, thus creating all sorts of "new" insights.  And so this movement, too, will pass into history as another example of what happens when you dishonor the Scriptures by mishandling them according to your own whims.

The cumulative effect of all of these groups and presentations is a general diminishment in the trust people believe they can put in the

Scriptures, because, they reason, "If so many people can read the same text and get so many different views from it, then who can really say for certain?" But this is a twisted way of thinking. Just because people abuse a text does not mean the text was not clear when it was written, nor does it mean we cannot get back to that meaning today. The phrase "separation of church and state" was clear when it was first written and in the context in which it was first written, and it had nothing at all to do with the restriction or prohibition of the free exercise of religious faith in the United States, nor did it at all suggest that in the public sphere religion had to be suppressed or hidden. But that phrase has been so often used in a different context, one directly contradictory to its original application, that one might be tempted to think its original use was ambiguous or unclear. It wasn't. Ignorance in the modern setting does not amount to a lack of clarity in the original.

**Tradition Trafficking**

By far the single greatest source of eisegesis in the preaching ministry finds its source in one word: tradition. Every minister comes to the pulpit out of a particular tradition. Even those who emphasize so strongly their independence and that they have "no creed but the Bible" have their own very strong traditions that directly impact their interpretation, preaching, and practice. Indeed, it must be understood by any and all that we each have our traditions, for unless we acknowledge this and identify how our tradition impacts our exegesis, we will surely allow those traditions to lead us right down the path to error.

It is not that we have not been warned about the danger of tradition already. The biblical writers were well aware of the penchant for man to create religious traditions that would before long override God's revelation in their lives, their worship, and their practice. The Lord Jesus fought constantly with the false accusations that flowed from the human traditions that had entered into the life of the Jewish people in His day. Even though they claimed their traditions had their origin in divine sources, the Lord knew otherwise:

> Then some Pharisees and scribes came to Jesus from Jerusalem and said, ² "Why do Your disciples break the tradition of the elders? For they do not wash their hands when

they eat bread." ³ And He answered and said to them, "Why do you yourselves transgress the commandment of God for the sake of your tradition? ⁴ "For God said, 'HONOR YOUR FATHER AND MOTHER,' and, 'HE WHO SPEAKS EVIL OF FATHER OR MOTHER IS TO BE PUT TO DEATH.' ⁵ "But you say, 'Whoever says to *his* father or mother, "Whatever I have that would help you has been given *to God*," ⁶ he is not to honor his father or his mother.' And *by this* you invalidated the word of God for the sake of your tradition. ⁷ "You hypocrites, rightly did Isaiah prophesy of you: ⁸ 'THIS PEOPLE HONORS ME WITH THEIR LIPS, BUT THEIR HEART IS FAR AWAY FROM ME. ⁹ 'BUT IN VAIN DO THEY WORSHIP ME, TEACHING AS DOCTRINES THE PRECEPTS OF MEN'" (Matthew 15:1-9)

Contrary to much of modern religious thought, just because religious men teach something does not mean that it is actually worthy of our respect. The Lord disrespected any doctrine or precept that pretended to lead men to worship of the true God that was, in fact, false, and that did not have its origin in God's own self-revelation. Such tradition "invalidates" or makes empty the word of God, though, of course, Jesus' opponents would have argued otherwise. They would have used all the same arguments we hear from the proponents of tradition today. They would have said it does not detract from but only adds to their experience of worship. They would have argued that their traditions came to them from reliable sources, and that they were fully in line with Scripture itself. What we learn from the Lord's words is not that we can ever pretend to be without tradition: as soon as we do something a second time in the church, we have created tradition. Instead, we learn from the Lord that we must always keep the order of authority in line: Scripture is God speaking. Tradition is examined by, and if necessary, rejected on the authority of, Scripture. One has full and final authority. The other is examined in light of divine revelation. Confuse the two and disaster results. Paul knew the devastation tradition could bring to the churches, for he warned the church at Colossae:

> See to it that no one takes you captive through philosophy and empty deception, according to the tradition of men, according to the elementary principles of the world, rather than according to Christ (Colossians 2:8).

Christ is the standard, and we know His truth through His word. But are there not positive references to tradition in Scripture? Yes, there are, but they are placed in a context that allows us to see the difference between the negative uses above, and the meaning of the writer when speaking positively of tradition. For example,

So then, brethren, stand firm and hold to the traditions which you were taught, whether by word *of mouth* or by letter from us. (2 Thessalonians 2:15)

Here we have a positive reference to tradition, do we not? Surely, but, in context, Paul is talking about the content of his teaching that had already been delivered to the saints both orally (through preaching), and by letter, that being 1 Thessalonians. In the immediately preceding context he was speaking of the gospel itself, which is what was delivered, and to which he called believers to hold fast (1 Cor. 16:13). So Paul is not here speaking of some external authority outside of Scripture and equal thereto, but to the very same apostolic truths found in inspired writ itself. So we have to examine the use of the term and recognize the different uses it bears in the Scriptures.

Some groups identified broadly as Christian openly embrace and promote the authority of tradition alongside Scripture. While recognizing the many texts that warn us about man's traditions they build an unbiblical theology from the positive references, and invariably, end up subsuming biblical teaching under the overarching authority of their traditions. The number of passages that must be "muted" by submission to the authority of tradition in the Roman Catholic system alone could easily fill a book, so the phenomenon is easy to document. But sadly, many self-proclaimed evangelicals, who would eschew fidelity to anything other than Scripture, are in reality just as bound to their own unspoken traditions as the most ardent supporter of the Papacy. In fact, one might argue that they are *more* bound to the authority of tradition because they refuse to acknowledge the presence of tradition at all. Instead, what happens is even more frightening in some instances, for then tradition ends up being viewed as if it is the word of God itself.

## Not Quite Being a Berean While Claiming to Be a Berean

My own work and ministry over the past number of years has provided me with the single greatest example of "slavery to tradition" I have ever encountered. I do hope to never have to examine another even clearer example.

A very well-known evangelical writer, whose books have literally sold millions of copies, chose to embark upon a campaign against Reformed theology. However, he chose to do so without first studying the issue he was addressing, and he did so from a position of holding to a very distinct set of traditional beliefs. I had the opportunity to challenging him on a drive-time radio program. In the course of the conversation he admitted he had never read a single book by the any of the Reformers, and he claimed he preferred to just "go with the Bible." But when we turned to the Bible, his exegesis was at best warped, clearly showing he was eisegetically reading his conclusions into the text of every verse presented to him. So finally at one point his comments were so far removed from the text under discussion I said, "That is just your tradition speaking." His response was, "James, I have no traditions."

Less than a year later this same writer produced a book attacking Reformed theology. The work was riddled with errors of fact, exegesis, history, and logic. But for our study of pulpit crimes, it provides us with a widely-distributed, easily documented example of what happens to one who claims to be founded directly on Scripture alone, who is given the pulpit in churches all across the world, and yet who proposes the grossest forms of eisegesis, all because of a stubborn refusal to acknowledge the role of tradition in his theology, and hence his identification of the conclusions of his tradition as God's truth itself. We can all learn a lesson from this kind of error, for this pulpit crime is one of the most common. In fact, these particular errors have been repeated over and over again by those who, because of their *traditional* agreement with this writer, take his writings to be *biblically* accurate, even if they do not take the time to verify these things for themselves. They then repeat these errors to their flocks, and the mere repetition becomes a self-validating means of promulgating the traditional belief at the expense of Scripture's actual teaching.

One of the first examples of eisegesis to be drawn from this writer has almost become classic, and would be rather humorous, if it were not so serious. We read in Acts 13:48:

> When the Gentiles heard this, they *began* rejoicing and glorifying the word of the Lord; and as many as had been appointed to eternal life believed.

This is not the foundational text of a belief in God's sovereignty in salvation, of course, as the final phrase is said in passing, and Reformed theology has never made it the cornerstone of its defense. However, it does reflect an understanding of the fact that belief is the result of God's ordination, God's ordering of events in time, His appointment. God's appointment is not the result of man's actions in time. This is directly contradictory to the standard post-evangelical concept of human autonomy and the priority of human actions to divine, the historic Calvinist/Arminian debate. Our writer has, over the past few years, offered almost every possible reinterpretation of this text in written form, even to the point of completely altering, without making notation of the changes, his published comments, removing certain arguments and providing completely contradictory ones in their place. At first he attempted to use the most common argumentation, which involves taking the translation in its most unusual possible interpretation, so that the Gentiles who believed did so because they had in essence "disposed themselves" to do so. This would require one to believe that even before hearing the gospel message, these particular Gentiles had disposed themselves to some kind of sensitivity to spiritual things. Whether this is possible is a question for many other texts of Scripture to address, but this is the commonly used means of trying to fit this text into a non-Reformed viewpoint. Though this writer denies any knowledge of the biblical languages, he offers numerous citations of scholarly sources (making errors of fact and context in the process), all to substantiate the reading, "as many [Greeks] as were *disposed* to eternal life believed." Evidently, he was unaware that there is, in fact, an English translation that provides this in its main text as its primary translation: the *New World Translation* published by the Watchtower Bible and Tract Society, the Jehovah's Witnesses, for there we read "all those who were rightly disposed to everlasting life became believers."

I pointed out the many self-contradictions and errors in this writer's presentation, and so in the next edition of the book, an almost entirely new section appeared in reference to Acts 13:48. Now, once again, when your interpretation of a text has been shown to be in error, what should be the believer's response? We do not simply find a new way to hold to the very same errors, do we? This would be the case only if our ultimate loyalty is to our traditions, not to the Scriptures. Sadly, in the new edition, without reference, this writer took out some of the blatant errors of fact that appeared in the previous edition, but replaced them with even *worse argumentation.* The most amazing new assertion provided to explain our writer's unwillingness to submit to the text is that the first fifteen chapters of Acts were written not in Greek anyway, but in Hebrew! He even alleges that the Dead Sea Scrolls teach this (a mighty incredible trick, given that the book of Acts was written *after* the DSS) and early church writers affirm this. However, when challenged once again to substantiate this assertion, our writer eventually had to admit he had no such evidence and that it was just "speculation" that would be removed from the next edition of the book. However, when that edition was released, the same material remained.

Surely, the lengths seen here utilized to get around the text might seem extreme. In my experience, they are in no way extreme for the person whose entire faith in Scripture is actually wrapped up in the defense of his traditions. This is why tradition trafficking must be recognized and dealt with early on. When a person spends their entire life in essence threading their own traditions into the very fabric of Scripture, there comes a time when they can no longer tell the difference between the two in even the strongest light. At this point the Scriptures have become compromised and their message mixed with a very non-divine voice. The results can be devastating especially when this person's traditions are proven false. They interpret this as an attack upon the entirety of Scripture itself, and either close their minds to correction, or, they completely lose faith.

Tradition trafficking has led our writer to a cavalier handling of many other texts of Scripture in service of his nearly canonized body of tradition. Sometimes it leads not so much to eisegesis as annihilation, the complete ignoring of a key text or passage that is contrary to the body of tradition the person has enshrined in their theology. For example, our writer often repeats the assertion that election is never to salvation, only to service. He wrote the entirety of his book repeating this assertion. Yet, nowhere in his book does he even make reference to 2 Thessalonians 2:13:

> But we should always give thanks to God for you, brethren beloved by the Lord, because God has chosen you from the beginning for salvation through sanctification by the Spirit and faith in the truth.

When faced with this reality, and the fact that it stands in direct contradiction to his oft-repeated theme, what does our slave of tradition do? He dismisses the text on the basis that it does not fit with God's character as seen "throughout Scripture." This isn't even eisegesis, as it does not even provide an attempt at handling the text in a meaningful fashion. The same comes out when the writer attempts to refute the assertion that 1 John 5:1 indicates that those who are believing (present tense, ongoing action) are doing so because they have, as a completed action in the past, been born of God. That is, being born of God (a divine action) leads to the ongoing exercise of faith on the part of the redeemed, a thoroughly Reformed concept. That is, true saving faith is the work of God in the heart that is part of His divine work of salvation, flowing from regeneration. Our writer rejects this out of hand, being a firm proponent of the autonomy of man and the freedom of his will.

In the case of 1 John 5:1, there are two parallel passages found in 1 John where the very same syntactical form appears (i.e., the grammar and relationship of the words found in these texts parallels that of 1 John 5:1). In 1 John 2:29 we read, "If you know that He is righteous, you know that everyone also who practices righteousness is born of Him." The same phrase, "born of Him," appears here, this time with the ongoing action of "the one doing righteousness." How are these related? Does the Christian "do righteousness" so as to become born of God, or does a Christian "do righteousness" because he or she has already been born of God, and that divine act gives rise to the human response? Likewise, in 1 John 4:10 we read, "Beloved, let us love one another, for love is from God; and everyone who loves is born of God and knows God." Here born of God is joined to "loving," again in a present-tense. Does a Christian love so as to become born again, or do they love because they have in fact already been born again, and it is the natural response of the regenerated soul to love? In each instance the writer is consistent. So how does our writer, the slave to tradition that he is, respond? Does he provide syntactical parallels? Exegetical insights from the surrounding context? In reality, the entirety of his response is summed up very easily. "It can be taken either way." No interaction with the text, no argumentation outside of saying, "Well, it just doesn't really matter."

The reader needs to keep in mind that in many other areas this writer would never, *ever* let someone get away with the kind of argumentation on, say, the resurrection, or the deity of Christ, that he himself uses here. It is that shift in hermeneutical method, that change in how you interpret the Bible, that is the clear indication that you have traditions that you are protecting from correction. You are tweaking the text to protect your tradition. The double standard *should* be clear to the person who is doing the interpretation, but, often, our closest held beliefs blind us to our own actions. That is one of the reasons, I believe, that God places a plurality of elders in the local church, for when one loses his balance, the others are to be there to help him regain it. When they see one of their own using different and contradictory methods of handling the Scriptures, they should rightly bring the attention before the entire group and address it. But while this is the ideal situation, many ministers find themselves alone, or virtually so, and are therefore without one of the aids God has intended for them to have. And authors are often not even elders themselves, or under the authority of elders, and are therefore prone to even wilder flights of fancy. This is surely the case with the author noted above. And the results are frightening.

## Honoring God, Honoring Scripture, Honoring Godly Traditions

There is a place for tradition in the Christian faith. It just needs to be the proper place. We do not, in fact, have to reinvent the faith with each generation. Anyone who thinks they have come to the faith without the influence of all the preceding generations impacting them is sorely mistaken, and those who wish to be free of all the godly insight and wisdom to be offered by those who have gone before are simply foolish. We need a heart of wisdom, to be sure, to separate the wheat from the chaff, the excellent from the shallow and misleading. It is not always easy. Sometimes we make a mistake. But it is part of the process to which we have been called.

I truly pity those who have no idea of the generations of faithful men and women who have lived before us in the grace of Christ. There is much encouragement to be gained by reading about their lives, their courage, their perseverance, and their suffering. We can learn much from their writings, gain great insights into the Scriptures, and learn how to apply Christian truth to our lives. But we dare not make them more than God intended them to be. They are not "God-breathed" as the Scriptures are. They can function as lights, sign-posts, but they cannot take the place of the word of God in our preaching and teaching. The body of insights derived from them, the traditions developed down through the ages, must be corrected by the Scriptures. Finding that balance requires first having one foot solidly on the ground laid out by our Lord Jesus Himself when He taught us to test all tradition, even that which is claimed to be divine, by the higher revelation of Scripture itself. Only then can we have a proper foundation for honoring God by not mixing with His voice the voice of uninspired men, and, at the same time, honoring truly godly tradition as it has come down to us in texts and practices that are commensurate with the divine revelation.

In all of this concern about exegesis, eisegesis, and tradition, what is most important is honoring God by allowing Him to speak with clarity. So many today wish to have God "speak," yet, He has already done so with finality in Christ, and in His Word. But to truly "hear" we must not interpose our traditions or our whims and desires between our God and His people, and that is what mishandling the Scriptures in the pulpit of the church does. All the hard work of rightly handling the Scriptures is just part of how the minister shows his love for God, for the Bible, and for the people he seeks to serve.

# CHAPTER TEN

## Cross Dressing

When Paul wrote to Timothy about how the church is to function in its regular life and ministry, he addressed key issues that are central to the health of the church down through the ages. He addressed, for example, the qualifications of elders, as we noted before. He laid out those qualifications so that generations long removed would be able to know Christ's will for His church. However, he only laid out qualifications for men to fulfill the position of elder. Further, in the apostolic example provided in Scripture, we only have direct, clear, incontrovertible evidence of male elders, not women elders. Brave attempts have been made to create grounds for such from passing references in the closing portions of some of the epistles, but if there were such office holders in the apostolic age, somehow, the Apostle forgot to provide qualifications for them in writing to both Timothy and Titus. Along with these lists of qualifications, the Apostle engaged in the following teaching when writing to Timothy:

> Likewise, *I want* women to adorn themselves with proper clothing, modestly and discreetly, not with braided hair and gold or pearls or costly garments, [10] but rather by means of good works, as is proper for women making a claim to godliness. [11] A woman must quietly receive instruction with entire submissiveness. [12] But I do not allow a woman to teach or exercise authority over a man, but to remain quiet. [13] For it was Adam who was first created, *and* then Eve. [14] And *it was* not Adam *who* was deceived, but the woman being deceived, fell into transgression (1 Tim. 2:9-14)

Paul is not in this text even addressing the issue of the eldership. In fact, Paul is addressing major groups in the churches and giving general outlines as to their proper behavior in the fellowship. When he turns to the women in the congregation, by even so doing, he is breaking with much of the tradition of the world around him. The high and exalted view of women as fellow image bearers and equals before God in the reception of the forgiveness of sins and eternal life was radical in its day. He addresses women "who make a claim to godliness," and gives instruction regarding their demeanor, their dress, the need for a focus upon the inward rather than the outward appearance. It is in this context of the inward, the spiritual, aspect of a godly woman's life that Paul states that she "must quietly receive instruction with entire submissiveness." Western culture, especially decadent Western culture, misses the point of this text as badly as most miss the real point of "Jacob I loved, Esau I hated" (the amazing statement there is not that God hated the reprobate Esau, but that He loved the equally evil Jacob!). In its context once again the exaltation of women is seen in Paul's instruction. In a day when women were little more than chattel, here he lays down an apostolic command that women are to be able to participate in the service of the church and, even more so, in the teaching ministry of the church, learning quietly and submissively. It is the fact that he lays down a principle that they are to do so in a way that adorns their profession of godliness that bothers many today. If a woman *learns* in silence, it follows she is not engaging in *teaching*. The submissive aspect would speak to both those teaching, and to the message taught, of course. But it is the implications of the silence (paralleled in 1 Cor. 14:34, "women are to keep silent in the churches") that leads then to the key text on the subject, verse 12.

The apostle, in speaking to Timothy, lays down a general rule. Now when we encounter such a rule, we ask if this rule was based upon merely cultural norms *by the writer himself* or if he founded his command upon something higher, something that transcends mere cultural standards. In this case there really is no question about how the Apostle viewed his command, placed in the first person ("I do not allow") that a woman not be allowed to teach or exercise authority over a man, but to remain quiet. His immediate grounding is found not in Greek societal norms, or even Hebrew/Jewish norms. He goes back to creation itself, to Adam and Eve. He refers to Adam's priority in creation, and Eve's priority in deception, in essence. Creative priority, and the woman's propensity to deception, are the Apostle's brief explanations of his apostolic example. We may speculate that he had expounded these concepts in a fuller fashion in Timothy's presence, but such speculation does not assist us in creating any fuller theology beyond what the text provides to us.

The text, then, seems to be quite clear in its meaning. In the context of handling the sacred truths within the teaching ministry of the church, Paul's apostolic practice was not to allow women to enter that role. Given that the very same apostle laid out as central to the work of the elder that very function of teaching, the vast majority of Christians down through the ages have concluded that women are not called into the ministry of authoritatively proclaiming the divine message in the ministry of preaching.

Of course, today, that majority opinion has been challenged. Many mainline denominations have concluded either that this text is completely conditioned upon culture, and hence is no longer relevant, or, more honestly, in my opinion, have dropped their view of the authority and nature of Scripture so low that their leaders and teachers are given the freedom to say, "I disagree with Paul." In any case, many women "priests" and "bishops" and "reverends" dot the religious landscape of post-evangelical Christendom in the West today. In my view, along with this change in view has come a greatly diminished view of the authority of preaching as well. The diminishment in authority may have led to, or assisted in the rise of, the egalitarian movement (the movement which seeks to create an equality between men and women in the church not just in redemptive contexts, but in service, ministry, and authority), but in any case, the two go hand in hand.

It is not my intention to go back over all the battles that have been fought over the past decades on this subject. The literature on the topic itself is now vast. Entire scholarly journals dedicated to just this one area of study are now in publication. In my view, there is a discernable difference in the view of Scripture espoused by the majority of those who oppose placing women in the eldership of the church and holding to established practice, and those who promote a female eldership. While some in that camp hold to a high view of Scripture, the majority do not, adopting cultural relativism or even lower views of inspiration. And historically, this movement has not led to a deepening of a denomination's commitment to foundational biblical truths, but has always been a part of a process of defection therefrom. While these issues are not exegetically relevant, they are nonetheless relevant to the wise of heart and observant of history.

If the pulpit is a place of authoritative proclamation, then we have little reason to come to any other conclusion than in God's economy, expressed by the Apostle, the woman is not invested with the authority, or the gifting by the Spirit, to do *all* that is required to fulfill that ministry. Please note I said *all*. So often this particular debate gets bogged down in personal stories about tremendously gifted women. "I knew a woman once who could preach circles around any man I've ever heard. She was incredible!" What does it mean to preach? In almost every instance, such a claim was focused solely upon the communicative aspects of preaching. She could speak clearly and had the ability to hold an audience. She might even have been able to tug at the heart strings. But all of this demonstrates a miserably shallow view of preaching in the first place. Yes, if one claims to be called to preaching it is a good idea to be able to talk your way out of a paper bag. But that is only part of the work. There is the right handling of divine truth. There is admonition, discipline, rebuke, and all of this consistently "in season and out of season." There is the proper exercise of authority, including bringing judgment to bear in the matter of church discipline. Now, the fact that many a man has failed in the face of men to properly follow through on all of these duties is not a relevant argument. The point is that God has His reasons for ordering His church as He sees fit, and in general, men are more suited for the wide range of activities related to the exercise of ministerial authority as defined by the New Testament. It is not that observation that substantiates the practice, however; the observation is merely made in a corroborating fashion. God can order His church as He wishes with or without our concession. It is His church, not ours, to order in the first place.

In the same fashion, our experience cannot be allowed to become normative of the proper ordering of Christ's church. I have heard many a prominent leader gush about a wonderful female teacher he encountered in his past, and clearly, it is that experience that has become normative for him, even to the point of providing that little extra push to adopt a hermeneutic on this particular topic that will allow him to get past 1 Timothy 2 and 1 Corinthians 14, grab hold of the exceptions and make out of them a rule, all the while undercutting the authoritative position of the pulpit in the church and, worse, in my opinion, the ability of the Bible to be seen as relevant to the actual definition of the Christian ministry in our day. While many who adopt this position do so out of an honest desire to "be sensitive to God's leading," there is something to be said for being firm in accepting God's decisions relating to how He will gift his people for service as well.

There are also a host of arguments to be wrestled with regarding lesser or derivative issues on this topic. What about the diaconate? What are the specific areas of ministry that would not involve the exercise of authoritative teaching by a woman over a man (Sunday School, women's Bible studies, etc.)? These are all excellent subjects for study, but they are often allowed to so cloud the central issue that the real problem is overlooked. Just as there is an order in creation, an order in the marriage relationship, there is an order in the ministries of the church. Despite the weight of Western culture today, God made men and women to differ from one another, and for good reasons. Part of the definition of the calling of the elder is to engage in discipline, rebuking, and the general exercise of authority in the shepherding of souls. God called men to those roles in the ancient church, and He did not indicate that he was going to alter His plans in the future. Unless we embrace continuing revelation, inspired tradition, or some other such mechanism of change, the wisdom of God should be allowed to stand.

### Pretty Pulpit Criminals

I have already shared my most memorable experience with a female pulpit criminal, the pretty blonde lady who could out-talk a chattering chipmunk who appears on "that network" that seems to specialize in lady preachers. I cannot imagine what kind of collection of pulpit crimes I could collect by watching that particular lady's "greatest hits" volumes. But she is just one of many in the media today. As I survey the landscape of female teachers/preachers, I come to an interesting conclusion: the majority I see are simply not orthodox. False teaching, in fact, seems *normative* for females. Think about it.  Consider all the great male preachers today from around the world, godly, orthodox men who hold firmly to the truth.  Now look at the leading females: word of faith teachers and preachers, many having obtained their position mainly through their less-than-orthodox husbands.  Oh, sure, there are still more male heretics than female ones, but if you just look at the women as a whole, the level of biblical orthodoxy in that group is barely discernable.  Could this have something to do with what Paul himself said long ago about Eve being deceived?  Could it be that once you loosen that one cord enough to allow yourself into the eldership a few other holes open up in the fabric that will allow all sorts of other things in?

No matter how one views the preceding discussion, one thing is for certain: wearing a dress does not keep you from joining the ranks of some of the worst pulpit criminals of all time.  While many of today's female false teachers do not bring in quite as much money as the "superstars" of pulpit crime (including the poofy-haired fellow who throws the Holy Spirit around his stadium conventions), they have certainly made a meteoric rise all the same.  Their books fill the shelves of "Christian" bookstores, they are seen on television daily, you can't miss them on "Christian" radio, and if you wait long enough, one of their caravans will slide into town to sell you health and wealth and success and beauty and acceptance...and even an exercise DVD!  Don't look for much in the way of sound theology, of course.  Normally you are getting a core of pop psychology buried in the skin of religiosity with a sprinkling of Christianity just to make it look respectable.  Sadly, desperate people with real problems turn to these teachers looking for truth, and instead get worldly philosophy and false religious teaching, and they think they are actually "trying" Christianity.  When it all fails, they become part of the great "religiously abused," a missions field fit only for the heartiest of souls.

But if you have looked at the current situation in our land, you have undoubtedly seen that the female pulpit criminal is judged much less harshly than her male counterpart.  It is almost as if we naturally know that she isn't really supposed to be there anyway, she isn't held to the same level of accountability, so who really cares if her Trinitarian theology is off a bit, her knowledge of the atonement defective?  She's just so good with those family issues!  And her stories about children are just adorable!  And so the "ends justifies the means" becomes the watchword and the purity of Christ's church and the integrity of His gospel suffer as a result.

Make no mistake. The female pulpit criminal will be just as accountable before God as any man, even more so given the biblical mandates regarding the qualifications of elders. Stepping into that office without divine calling and divine authority is a high crime and misdemeanor to be sure. Only when we think that God is not concerned about our honoring of his ordering of the church will we think that He will pass over this kind of pulpit crime lightly.

# CHAPTER ELEVEN

## Body Count

"I don't need to be a member of a church. I can worship God in many places, and in many churches. I can serve Him as I see fit." So goes the modern mantra, and so we have the modern scene in post-evangelicalism: the church-hopping believer who is always looking for the best music, the best preacher, the best set of programs to "meet my needs." And there is a never ending supply of churches ready to join the marketing campaign, always seeking to appeal to this kind of wandering spirit.

It has not always been like this. In days past one believed it a duty to not only attend church but to do so consistently as part of one's ministry to Christ. There was a sense of community, of belonging, that even led to the idea of serving one another and learning to get along with even those who are not exactly like you in your thinking or culture. But this was before the church and those in its fellowship lost sight of such weighty issues as God-centeredness, God's right to define worship, and the call to service that is part of Christian discipleship. Now everything is geared toward the "seeker," the "worshiper" (instead of the one worshiped), and the fulfillment of "felt needs."

As a result, the idea of church membership is fast fading from the modern landscape. Membership rolls are seen by many as restrictive. How can we attract our "prospects" when we might frighten them off with talk of membership and duties and the like? And to be honest, in many churches that still continue the practice, what good are the rolls anyway? It is a standing joke in many churches that a person must die, and personally present their death certificate, in triplicate, to be taken off the rolls anyway. Members of "mega-churches" well know the gap that exists between the huge numbers of "members" and the actual number of people who attend in with any kind of regularity. Everyone knows, but few want to discuss, the huge number of nominal "Christians" in post-evangelical churches today who were once baptized, once made profession of faith, but have not darkened the door of the church in the past number of years. Their spiritual state is unknown, so whether they are lost sheep, wandering and in danger without a shepherd, or were never sheep to begin with, but false professors who have gotten over the financial/personal/medical crisis that prompted a brief flirtation with religion, no one can say. They are the great unpaid debt of the church, a fertile ground for cults and isms to gain new converts.

What you win them with is what you win them to. The man-centered gospel of post-evangelicalism, not surprisingly, produces man-centered converts who have no interest at all in being "stuck" in one church by rules and duties and covenants. If a better show comes into town, why shouldn't we all be free to go there? We have freedom of religion, after all! Isn't there something fundamentally wrong about *limiting* religious options? And what if I feel that my "needs" will be met better elsewhere? Can't I just up and leave? As long as folks have come into their religious experience with the idea that they are in charge and God is just simply *fortunate to have them*, we can hardly be surprised when they consistently transfer that thought into the area of church membership and accountability.

### But...is it Biblical?

I have indeed encountered many who have questioned the propriety of church membership by claiming there is no evidence for the practice or idea within the Scriptures themselves. And surely we will come up empty if we go looking for the phrase in the Bible, at least in its modern form. While we can, in fact, discern lists or records in the Old Testament with reference to priests and genealogies and the like, we see no explicit reference to someone standing by during the mass baptisms of Pentecost writing down address information and explaining the church membership covenant to the new converts. There is no call for believers to be faithful to the commitments made "to the church" or to a particular local congregation in the Bible. So why should anyone even consider the idea that church membership is, in fact, proper?

The answer can be provided in a number of ways. There is no question that there is no such thing as a Lone Ranger Christian, a believer God intends to wander about in life without any fellowship with other believers. While in some rare circumstances a Christian may have almost no other Christians around them, in the majority of instances one can, in fact, find fellowship, and there seems to be good evidence that the early Christians worked very hard at finding ways of creating those fellowships, leading to the establishment of formal churches. The Scriptures speak often of Christians gathering for worship, prayer, and proclamation, and it is rather clear that there was a form to this worship, as laid out in Acts and in the pastoral epistles. Fellowship, and the resultant responsibilities for interpersonal behavior, including forgiving one another, bearing one another's burdens, and the like, imply strongly that you were meeting with the same folks over time. If you were hopping about from one group to another, you would never have to go through that messy process of actually getting along with others in your fellowship. Instead of urging Euodia and Syntyche (Phil. 4:2) to live in harmony, Paul could have just suggested one of them move on to a different fellowship. Why worry about all this harmony stuff if things could be so fluid, so free-flowing?

More directly to the issue is the reality that the New Testament speaks of church discipline, of putting people out of the fellowship for reasons of immorality, apostasy, and false teaching. It is hard to put someone "out" when you can't define what it means to be "in." If the church has no walls, no definition, no identity as to who is, and who is not, a part of its fellowship, the entire discussion of church discipline, apostasy, and the like, is, of course, irrelevant. As John the beloved apostle could opine, undoubtedly with sadness, but with an eye to the reality that the church would always face difficulties, "They went out from us, but they were not *really* of us; for if they had been of us, they would have remained with us; but *they went out*, so that it would be shown that they all are not of us" (1 John 2:19). Went out? You have to have defined parameters to make sense of such language. There had been fellowship, now, that fellowship was broken. There was something about "them" and "us" that could not allow "both" to remain as one. Surely this shows us that there were recognizable boundaries, and this is still in the days when Christianity was a small minority, a persecuted few. We also see that these boundaries were not only geographical, they were more importantly theological in nature.

But the strongest argument I know regarding the biblical nature of church membership is probably the most obvious. What are the duties of elders? We can find their qualifications listed by Paul in writing to Timothy and Titus (1 Timothy 3:1-7, Titus 1:5-11) and from these glean much about their duties. And we have the plain statement of Peter,

> Therefore, I exhort the elders among you, as *your* fellow elder and witness of the sufferings of Christ, and a partaker also of the glory that is to be revealed, [2] shepherd the flock of God among you, exercising oversight not under compulsion, but voluntarily, according to *the will of* God; and not for sordid gain, but with eagerness; [3] nor yet as lording it over those allotted to your charge, but proving to be examples to the flock (1 Peter 5:1-3).

The argument is simple: *shepherds must know their sheep to be able to fulfill their duties as shepherds.* It's just that simple. You cannot "shepherd the flock of God" when you haven't a clue who the flock of God is. Every good shepherd knows his sheep. Only the hireling does not know the identity of the members of the flock. And, of course, the relationship is mutual. The sheep know their shepherd. They will not listen to another's voice because they have been with the one shepherd so long they know his voice over against any pretenders or strangers. Such involves a relationship over time, just as the Christian elder is not to be a hireling, some "young gun" brought in from outside, but should be one who ideally fulfills the commandment of Paul, "The things which you have heard from me in the presence of many witnesses, entrust these to faithful men who will be able to teach others also" (2 Timothy 2:2). The gospel is something that is precious, and you *entrust* it to the next generation. But it is the elders who make this decision, as they have to decide just who is truly "faithful" and who has the ability to teach others. All of this requires community, exposure, contact, once again demonstrating that the shepherd must have direct knowledge of the sheep who have been entrusted to his care.

Further, Peter speaks of exercising oversight. While we may discuss the exact nature of what this means (and allow for differences given culture and geography and the like) one thing is for certain: it cannot be done without a relationship of some kind that involves "real life." Obviously, this involves teaching and exhortation and discipline on the part of the elder. He is to be an example. You cannot be an example from a distance. You cannot be an example through a television screen or through the pages of a book. Modeling Christian maturity takes contact, exposure, and a reciprocal relationship that involves at least some kind of personal, communal, corporate context. All of this proves that despite the lack of the specific term "membership rolls" (something that would have been pretty dangerous at that point in time anyway), the activities of the elders and the form of the church itself require one to see the necessity of commitment to a particular fellowship identifiable by a particular group of elders. And if these texts were not enough, surely this command to all obedient Christians should be:

> Obey your leaders and submit *to them*, for they keep watch over your souls as those who will give an account. Let them do this with joy and not with grief, for this would be unprofitable for you (Hebrews 13:17).

Here the Christian duty of obedience and submission, coupled with a need to make this work on the part of the elders of the congregation one of joy rather than grief, is enjoined upon all. This is not a command to servility, nor does it grant to Christian leaders despotic powers. But it does require believers to know who their leaders are. It is empty to say, "Jesus is my leader!" for the writer to the Hebrews did not say "your Leader" but "your leaders," plural, and he would distinguish between them and the Great Shepherd only a few lines later (13:20). Nor does it do to claim to be in obedience and submission to men who do not see your face but once or twice a year. How can they "give an account" when they have no meaningful knowledge of your life, your Christian experience, your growth in godliness? How can they do so when you never attend upon their teaching or encounter them in the congregation?

And so we see in this brief review that the church has a self-identity. The elders know the sheep committed to their care, the sheep know their elders, and so we have church membership. Of course, all of this is based upon the idea that Scripture is actually sufficient to set the norm for the church and that as a result we can affirm a divine institution called the church that is being built by Christ to the glory of the triune God, which is a glorious truth far too often ignored in the preaching and teaching ministry of the church today. Without a high view of Scripture and the church, these issues become, in general, irrelevant. But given these foundational truths, we can move to the nature of this "pulpit crime."

### Shopping Center Church

Surely many a pastor well knows how his job would be far different in nature if there was a consistent, interested, spiritually aware, spiritually prepared group of saints before him as he pours out his heart in delivering the message of God from the Word at the stated meetings of the church. But the reality is that more often than not he is facing a small core of regular attendees along with a much broader group of "hit and miss" folks. For only a small number can he even attempt to lay a foundation in his preaching and then build upon it. If he tries to do this in most situations he will inevitably leave the inconsistent folks behind. He will be accused of not being "caring" or being too "complex."

Of course, in many churches today, the real pulpit crime is even worse, and it takes place on both sides of the pulpit! You have those in leadership who have so thoroughly embraced an unbiblical view of the church and its purposes that they form the entirety of their ministry so as to pander to the worst instincts of those seeking to meet some "felt religious need." From the very pulpit the church is "marketed" as a product to be consumed by the eager throngs. The gospel is sugarcoated so that the offense to the natural man is removed and great effort is put into making this particular "reseller" more attractive than the one down the street. Programs and entertainment and the like become the "product" to be packaged and sold each and every Sunday, and the "ministers" become the salesmen.

But this crime goes both ways. Those sitting in front of the pulpit are just as guilty. If they were not "in the market" and hence unfaithful to the calling of God's Spirit to service in a definable, identifiable congregation of Christ's people, there would be no reason for those ministers to be prostituting themselves and the gospel and the church the way they are. You have to have customers to keep a store open, and once the church becomes a marketplace, it has to keep looking for more and more customers to buy its goods. Whenever a self-professed believer is "church hopping" around, looking for the newest show, the best entertainment, you can be sure you have here a person, a family, called to service in a particular place who is missing the blessing of obedience, just as the others in that congregation are missing their ministry. Yes, ministry. When you are faithful in attendance upon God's Word in the midst of God's people, you minister to the others by your consistency. You especially minister to the faithful servant who brings the Word in sermon and exhortation. But this is not the case with the church hopper who does little more than window-shop down the main street of evangelicalism. There can be no ministry to others when no one there has a clue who you are. There can be no ministry to the pastor when he is not actually your shepherd and would not recognize you if he saw your picture on the Post Office wall. In short, *this just isn't Christian ministry and worship*. You may get warm fuzzies during the service, but you can get warm fuzzies in a movie theater. You cannot, however, fulfill Christ's command to "love the brethren" and "bear one another's burdens" and "forgive one another" when you are not a regular, faithful member of a local church *when you have the ability to do such*. Do not use the rare situation where believers are far removed from others as an excuse. The Lord knows your heart as He knows mine, and He knows if we are truly hindered by His providence from gathering with the saints or whether we simply lack a true love for the brethren.

### Boasting of Ghosts

There are many other aspects to this particular realm of pulpit crimes, but we shall only examine one more. It is a true pulpit crime in that it is seen in the boasting done by some concerning the size of their congregations. Oh, it is always couched in the "look what the Lord has done for us, aren't we grateful" language that we Christians are so good at using to cover over our boasting. But the pride is still there. And the worst part of the boasting is this: in the vast majority of cases where you hear about "our 15,000 members" or the like, *the church couldn't locate half those folks if their lives depended on it.* I have actually been in churches that boasted 20,000 members but had, at best, 8,000 in attendance on any given Sunday, and when the truth was told, could not locate a good third of that huge, bloated membership roll. Shepherds with flocks that large are in deep trouble, but, of course, the probability is high that most of those "sheep" are not sheep at all to begin with, but false professors who assuaged their guilt one day by doing something "religious" and immediately returned to their self-centered life of indulgence.

But this pulpit crime can be made all the more heinous when the ordinances of the Lord become means by which "church growth numbers" are inflated. It is a very sad truth that in many mega-churches today of the Baptist bent you can find people who have been baptized two and three times, each at different stages of their lives, *and all those baptisms have been reported to the central denomination as individual baptisms counting toward a yearly total.* For many of these churches, they must "baptize" literally dozens of people to get a *single* faithful worshipper of Christ who could in any way even come close to resembling the portrait of a Christian found in such inspired documents as the First Epistle of John or the Epistle of James. And what of the majority who go away from that building thinking themselves religious and right with God? Are not those indulging in this pulpit crime guilty of complicity in producing those who will someday do as Jesus said?

> "Many will say to Me on that day, 'Lord, Lord, did we not prophesy in Your name, and in Your name cast out demons, and in Your name perform many miracles?' [23] "And then I will declare to them, 'I never knew you; DEPART FROM ME, YOU WHO PRACTICE LAWLESSNESS' (Matthew 7:22,23)

# CHAPTER TWELVE

## Identity Theft

### The Abuse of the Gracious Gifts of the Ordinances of the Church

**Matthew 28:18-20** [18] And Jesus came up and spoke to them, saying, "All authority has been given to Me in heaven and on earth. [19] Go therefore and make disciples of all the nations, baptizing them in the name of the Father and the Son and the Holy Spirit, [20] teaching them to observe all that I commanded you; and lo, I am with you always, even to the end of the age."

**1 Corinthians 11:23-26** For I received from the Lord that which I also delivered to you, that the Lord Jesus in the night in which He was betrayed took bread; [24] and when He had given thanks, He broke it and said, "This is My body, which is for you; do this in remembrance of Me." [25] In the same way *He took* the cup also after supper, saying, "This cup is the new covenant in My blood; do this, as often as you drink *it*, in remembrance of Me." [26] For as often as you eat this bread and drink the cup, you proclaim the Lord's death until He comes.

The ordinances of the church. History has recorded many controversies and arguments over their nature and importance, and possibly, because of this, many in the modern church hold them at arm's length, showing little concern about them and less interest in considering the wisdom of God displayed in them. And yet generations past have placed great weight upon these ordinances, or, as some prefer, sacraments, pointing out rightly that it was Christ Himself who gave them to His church. If our Lord chose to bless

His people with these gifts of grace, should we not hold them in the highest esteem? Should we not rejoice in them, find great comfort in them, and take great encouragement from participating in the gathered body as we observe baptism and as we join together in our common proclamation of the Lord's death until He comes?

Let us briefly consider these two ordinances, and then consider how often they are the subject of pulpit crime in our day.

### Baptism: Sign and Seal of Our Union with Christ

Since the ordinances set the Christian church apart from the religions around it and hence have been part of Christian worship from the start, it is hardly surprising that every kind of controversy has erupted over time regarding them. Baptism has been viewed in many ways, sometimes for centuries on end in very unbiblical fashions. And as much as some would like to avoid controversy, the fact is baptism is right there in front of us in the text of Scripture, so what it means, and how it relates to our understanding of the gospel and the church, cannot be avoided. We may simply collapse into the arms of past generations and not struggle with the issue ourselves, adopting the traditions of others as our own, or we may learn from those struggles, stand on the shoulders of giants, and once again look with sincere desire to the Word of God for understanding.

I address baptism as a convinced covenantal credobaptist, a rare enough creature I admit. That is, as a Reformed Baptist elder, I believe baptism "is an ordinance of the New Testament, ordained by Jesus Christ, to be unto the party baptized, a sign of his fellowship with him, in his death and resurrection; of his being engrafted into him; of remission of sins; and of his giving up unto God, through Jesus Christ, to live and walk in newness of life" (*London Baptist Confession of Faith, 1689,* 29:1). I can only speak with passion of baptism in this context. I do not believe baptism regenerates, but is for the regenerate only. I do not believe it unites with Christ, but instead pictures that union that exists between the believer and Christ. It is a sign of our fellowship with Christ in His death and resurrection, for it is associated with our dying to our old selves and living in newness of life. When we consider our baptisms, this should come to our minds, that we have died, and our life is hidden with Christ in God (Col. 3:3). The confession we gave in our baptisms should go with us throughout our lives, and we should often be asking the Lord to rekindle that fire we had as we stood publicly, unashamed to be associated with Christ.

Our baptism speaks to our union with Christ. As we undergo this ordinance, we stand in the line of millions who have gone before us in confessing the same faith in the same Lord. Just as those saints before us were joined to Him, so too we have experienced the work of God's Spirit in being drawn by the Father to the Son. We bear His mark, we confess His faith, we are united with Him in death, burial and resurrection. There is no aspect of our lives untouched by this union, and this is why it should not only be precious to us in its initial experience, but it should be something to which our minds turn with regularity as we again recall with joy the work of God in our lives.

Our baptism openly professes our belief that Christ's death, burial, and resurrection is the *sole* means of redemption, of the remission of sins. The rite pictures this reality, but it most assuredly does not accomplish this reality. Indeed, it is a true profanation of the truth of baptism to confuse it with the reality it represents. It is Christ's death, and our union with Him in the sovereign grace of God that effects redemption (Eph. 1:7), not the action of baptism. Baptism looks back to an accomplished reality; it does not at that time save, nor does it merely look forward to a hoped-for fulfillment. What it pictures in its context and mode was accomplished through God's power (without our aid and assistance) and we are the recipients of His powerful gracious work in the gospel.

When we consider what God has done for us in Christ, we see in our baptism our unreserved giving up of ourselves to Him. We do not baptize ourselves, we are baptized, fully under the control of another. Likewise we are now disciples of Christ, followers, to be used in service to Him. He has commanded that we be baptized, and we are obeying, and will continue to obey, as faithful disciples.

Baptism is not just an individual activity. The church baptizes as part of her commission. The church observes these confessions of faith, the church embraces those thusly baptized. Baptism is one of the means God has given His church to establish and propagate the community of faith. Our baptisms bind us together as part of our profession of faith. Baptism nourishes the sense of community, and as such is a vital part of the means of grace God has given us as we seek to faithfully serve Him.

**Proclaim His Death**

The sure approach of death focuses one's mind like nothing else. Our Lord, knowing full well what was coming upon Him, took great pains to establish for his disciples a memorial supper, a time when they could, as a gathered body, partake of the meal and in so doing "remember" Him. It was important to our Lord, it should be just as important to us today. And yet for many, it is but a ritual with little direct impact upon their faith and their spiritual life.

Once again looking to my own community's confession of faith, we are told,

> The supper of the Lord Jesus was instituted by him the same night wherein he was betrayed, to be observed in his churches, unto the end of the world, for the perpetual remembrance, and shewing forth the sacrifice of himself in his death, confirmation of the faith of believers in all the benefits thereof, their spiritual nourishment, and growth in him, their further engagement in, and to all duties which they owe to him; and to be a bond and pledge of their communion with him, and with each other. (*LBCF* 30:1)

If even half of the claims of this confession of faith are true, one would expect believers to be flocking to attend to this divine source of assistance and grace. Books would be filling our shelves on the subject, and being excluded from the Lord's table would be a grave punishment indeed. The fact that even consistently attending to the Lord's table, however often it is offered in one's fellowship, is about as high a priority as bringing the donuts to Sunday School or a covered dish to the fellowship meal after hymn sing, evidently what we *say* we believe in our confessions is a mile away from the actual practice of most. But honesty demands we ask: how can we avoid being convicted of ignoring, to a great extent, Christ's own wisdom in ordering His church if we do not in fact accept His own command to observe, to our own great benefit, this ordinance?

The confession goes on to deny, rightfully, the excesses of the Roman Catholic system in turning the memorial of Christ's death into a re-presentation of the sacrifice of Christ so that it becomes, in fact, a propitiatory, but never perfecting, sacrifice. But while it denies that any "real sacrifice" is made in the Lord's Supper, it interestingly (and shockingly, for some Baptists), says that the supper is "only a memorial of that one offering up of himself by himself upon the cross, once for all; and a spiritual oblation of all possible praise unto God for the same" (*LBCF* 30:2). Spiritual oblation of all possible praise? For many, the Supper is nothing more than a brief period of self-reflection punctuated by grape juice and a cracker. But it is much more than that.

Two elements of Paul's words to the Corinthians would help many believers appreciate more deeply the theology of the Supper. First, Jesus Himself defined the nature of His own memorial: "do this in remembrance of Me." This is a command, not a suggestion, establishing the divine nature of the institution. But it is the nature of "remembrance" that needs to be kept in mind. Remembrance is not something that is a major portion of most Western cultures, but it is far more central in ancient cultures of the past. Engaging in particular activities, often in a regular fashion, was a means of connecting the current generation to past generations. Remembering those who came before us helps us to see ourselves as part of something larger than ourselves. Remembrance makes those who lived before "real" to us now.

The Lord's words go beyond mere recollection of past heroes. Christ is the risen Lord, the One who by His Spirit indwells His people. So when we obey His command to "remember" Him, we are doing much more than just recalling facts about the past. He is present with us in His body at all times, and never more so than when we are portraying, by our actions (breaking the bread, drinking the cup), our confession that it is solely, completely, and wholly by *His* work that we are redeemed, solely to *His* glory. We stand forgiven as members of the New Covenant in His blood, and by partaking of the supper we are remembering the means by which that covenant was enacted, through the broken body and shed blood of the perfect Savior.

This concept of remembrance is deepened when we contrast the use Jesus makes of "remembrance" *of Him* with the only other reference to the term in the New Testament, found in Hebrews chapter ten:

> For the Law, since it has *only* a shadow of the good things to come *and* not the very form of things, can never, by the same

sacrifices which they offer continually year by year, make perfect those who draw near. ² Otherwise, would they not have ceased to be offered, because the worshipers, having once been cleansed, would no longer have had consciousness of sins? ³ But in those *sacrifices* there is a reminder of sins year by year. ⁴ For it is impossible for the blood of bulls and goats to take away sins (Hebrews 10:1-4).

Here the writer to the Hebrews is contrasting the once-for-all, finished, final sacrifice of Christ with the old covenant sacrifices that were repeated over and over again. The sacrifice on the Day of Atonement is particularly in view. Each year the people were called to make sacrifice, and this repeated activity was a *reminder*, a *remembrance* (same term as that used by Jesus) not of a Savior, *but of their sins*. The repetitive nature showed the imperfection of the sacrifice. It is just this that we do *not* have in the New Covenant! We have a reminder, a remembrance, not of sin, but of a Savior who has perfectly removed our sin by taking our place upon the cross of Calvary. It should be a singular cause of abiding joy to recall this truth in the Supper.

The second truth to see in Paul's words is one that has truly been lost for many today. Paul taught, "For as often as you eat this bread and drink the cup, you proclaim the Lord's death until He comes." Believers are *active* in the Supper. For so many we just sit like a lump on a log, introspective, eat a cracker, drink a little cup, sing a hymn, go home. We do not see that we are *doing* something, something of eternal value. We are *proclaiming* something. These words are addressed to *all* who in faith participate, not just to the elders, not just to the preacher. Everyone is proclaiming the Lord's death until He comes. We are doing so by faith. By partaking we are saying, "Yes, this is the source of my life, this is how I've been redeemed, by the giving of the body and blood of Jesus Christ in my stead." We are saying this to ourselves. We are saying this to all those around us. We are joining a group of believers who are all likewise solemnly confessing this faith. We are standing in an unending line of believers who have been drawn out of the world and united with Christ and granted the same faith all across the spectrum of time, geography, and culture. We are making sure by our actions that what happened on a windswept hill outside of Jerusalem so long ago will never, as long as the sun rises and sets, be forgotten. This is our privilege, this is our calling, this is our gift of grace in the Lord's Supper.

This, then, is why my confession of faith can refer to the Supper as a "spiritual oblation of all possible praise unto God" for Christ's sacrifice upon the cross. We are to prepare for the Supper, consider the meaning of the Supper, look forward to it, and contemplate with joy and gratitude the awesome self-sacrificing love that has brought us true and lasting peace with God.

## The Abuse of the Ordinances

Baptism, as the initiatory rite of the Christian faith, is the most easily abused in our modern context. The frequent perversion of its meaning leading to a false trust in the rite itself, rather than true and repentant faith in Christ, is one of the greatest "pulpit crimes" of the entire history of the church. How many have died and entered a Christ-less eternity trusting in a baptism that meant nothing more than their becoming wet? This will always remain the worst pulpit crime committed regarding baptism: replacing the Bible's clear call for heartfelt repentance and faith in Christ with what is actually the first act of obedience on the part of the believer, his appeal to God for a good conscience (1 Peter 3:21), baptism itself.

Recognizing how serious that is, we must honestly turn the spotlight upon many who would never direct us to baptism as a means of salvation, but who still offend seriously against God's truth through their abuse of the ordinance of baptism. I refer to the shallow, surface-level use of baptism as a means to fill the pews, impress the denominational headquarters, and pump up the membership rolls.

There is a fine line between being very concerned about the souls of our people and hence desiring to see them converted and baptized, and the crass use of baptism to meet a particular goal over a specific period of time. The one can far too often be covered over with the profession of the other. Anyone who has endured the end-of-the-year push to meet a goal of baptisms for the year knows well what takes place. Entire sermons on baptism, all aimed at getting as many bodies through the baptistery as possible, along with "bring a friend" drives, all end up producing what can only be called Christian mutations: baptism without conversion, religiosity without repentance, non-discipled disciples, moistened, but now guilty of religious hypocrisy as well. The numbers may look good, but what do they really represent?

Some of the largest, conservative denominations are particularly guilty of inspiring this pulpit crime in their ministers and churches. The rampant assumption that the work of the Spirit of God can be plotted on graphs and charts has created an entire mind-set that refuses to recognize God's own sovereignty over His church and that it is the Lord, not man, that adds to the church daily those who are being saved (Acts 2:47). The idea that God could actually have a purpose in a church with a growth rate less than double digits but where He is praised in purity, His truth is proclaimed with clarity, and those in the fellowship are growing in the grace and knowledge of the Lord Jesus Christ, needs to be championed once again. "Church growth" can become an idol when viewed outside the balance of God's Word just as any other good and proper concept. While the church should never be complacent about the proclamation of the gospel and the salvation of sinners, in many places today, that singular goal has become the *only* calling of Christ's people, and that concept cannot be substantiated by a fair reading of Scripture.

The "numbers" mentality has resulted in egregious abuses of baptism at the hands of ostensibly orthodox men. In recent years a large church in the United States became known for having a children's baptismal service featuring the firing of cannons with confetti and lights and a siren going off when the child was baptized. Though the church later attempted to put a biblical spin upon this blight on their reputation, the fact remains that the only reason such a concoction ever saw the light of day was to seek to encourage young folks to make a profession of faith followed by baptism. We are truly brought back to a fundamental question by such out-of-balance practices: who saves, and for what purposes? Those who make human autonomy and free will definitive of their theology have little consistent basis for avoiding such excesses, but those who rest upon the sovereignty of God and His divine ordination of both the ends as well as the means are in a position to do honor to all of the biblical revelation. A child drawn to baptism out of a desire to be baptized is being put in spiritual danger for the rest of his or her life. Those who have had "their tickets punched" and have been assured, mistakenly, of their eternal salvation solely due to something *they* did, a card they filled out, a prayer they recited, are some of the hardest people in the world to reach with a real message of repentance and faith. It is a pulpit crime indeed to encourage such shallow "conversionism" that is not born in the heart by a mighty work of the Spirit of God resulting in repentance and faith in Christ.

An example from my own experience will always remain fresh in my mind. I was in attendance at one such push for baptisms at a very large evangelical church a few decades ago. The entire service was focused upon getting as many people as possible into the baptistery at the end of the service (and it just so happened the church reporting year ended the next weekend). Fifty or sixty people made the trek upstairs to the font, and we all dutifully stayed in our pews to observe the lengthy service. Of course, a grand total of possibly ten minutes had passed between the time when these people "came forward" and when they entered the waters, so these folks were operating on nothing more than the instruction found in the sermon itself, which was hardly in-depth, and was focused primarily on baptism, not upon the theology of the gospel. As the people filed through the baptistery, a woman came down to be baptized. The pastor was standing behind, preparing to baptize her, quoting the standard formulary he used to do so. He could not see that the woman, right as he was about to baptize her, crossed herself in typical Roman Catholic fashion. The entire congregation could see it, even the television cameras caught it, but the pastor had no idea. Now surely, this woman could have been a life-long Roman Catholic who had just been converted and was simply going on instinct, and I like to hope and pray that is the case. But, it is just as likely, if not more so, that the woman had no concept whatsoever of what that church professed to believe nor how that was relevant to her faith as a Roman Catholic. She was simply doing something religious. And given that I later learned that in that particular congregation 83% of all those baptized were simply "gone," without contact, without connection, within a year of their baptism, that is probably what happened in that situation.

I fully understand that, thankfully, only a small number of men actually go into the ministry thinking they will use it to their own ends and will happily abuse even the ordinances of the church as long as it leads to their own satisfaction and self-aggrandizement.

Even some of the worst examples of ordinance abuse came about because of a slow and all-too-common process. The young minister goes into his task with high motives, but, he is not alone in the fellowship. He is under pressure from those in his church to meet certain expectations, some of which are not godly nor are they biblically founded. There is the pressure of other ministers in his association or denomination. There is the inevitable comparison of his "success" in ministry with those in his area, down the street, across the town. At first the compromises do not seem that major, just small matters of "freedom." The initial step down the path may be quite defensible in some contexts. "It won't hurt to do this one little thing, we have the right motivations." But then that is followed by another small step, and another small step, and eventually the now-compromised minister finds himself staring at a situation he never dreamed would come to fruition in his experience. What began with good motivations but which still involved a "minor" infraction of God's revealed will ends up a full-blown pulpit crime, and once again God's wisdom in revealing His will with clarity is vindicated.

### The Supper Marginalized, Trivialized

The primary "pulpit crime" relating to the Lord's Supper is well known, that being Rome's transformation of the memorial of a finished work and a perfect Savior into an on-going re-presentation that perfects no one and a Savior who tries real hard but is unable to save outside of human cooperation. Sadly, many Protestant denominations, especially those that have a deep sacramental streak running through their traditions, tiptoe along that line as well.

In the broad spectrum of the post-evangelical world, however, the primary pulpit crime relating to the Supper is simple apathy. In some places it is observed so rarely that it can hardly command any serious attention. In others, it is so regularly observed that it becomes a mere part of the "routine." But in so many churches today the average congregant, even the one who attends to the ministry regularly, cannot give you a meaningful theology of the Supper and cannot relate the ordinance to any aspect of their Christian lives. If we were to exclude from the celebration of the Supper a large portion of those who attend, they would not even miss the event, and this says much about the marginalization of this Christ-ordained event.

Why is there such little passion about this ordinance? I dare say it is mainly because of the shallow depth of the post-evangelical church's doctrines of sin and atonement. When "the old rugged cross" is as deep as you dare to go in developing your own theology of the cross, a remembrance of that event, along with the related topics of the New Covenant, the mercy seat, the extent and intention of the atonement, etc., is hardly going to commend itself. If we are satisfied with surface level treatments of the great themes of Scripture (hard to do much more than that when your church growth manual tells you to limit your sermons to 20 minutes so that the praise and worship team has enough time to do all their special numbers) and of the gospel surely we will not want to invest a lot of effort in mining the treasures discoverable in the Lord's Supper. Only when we have a solid view of the wonder of God's grace, the centrality of Christ, and the love displayed in Christ's self-sacrifice, will we begin to see how important it is that we "remember" the Lord's death until He comes. As long as we see ourselves as quite lovable and quite worthy of such sacrifice, we will not appreciate Christ's work, or our remembrance of it, properly.

There is one other aspect of this issue I would like to address, and I do so knowing that I will be offending many readers. Almost everyone I know practices, in a sense, "closed baptism." That is, we seek a confession of faith, a reliance upon Christ, a knowledge of the meaning of the ordinance, before administering it to someone. I speak here, of course, as a convinced credobaptist, not as a paedobaptist. Yet for some reason the Supper seems to be viewed as a free-for-all, a general rite that anyone can engage in without question. I recognize that there are a number of thorny issues that arise when we seek to protect this practice and limit participation to those who confess the name of Christ and hence can discern the body and blood of the Lord as redeemed individuals. But shouldn't we at least make the attempt to honor this ordinance in light of the biblical commands that accompany it? Are we so afraid of the face of men that we are not willing to ask for the most basic confession of faith before admitting someone to this precious ordinance?

There is another aspect related to this consideration that is rarely considered. If we do not seek to inquire as to the state of the soul of those who come into our fellowship and seek to participate in the ordinance of the Lord's Supper, how can church discipline ever have any meaning? If all I have to do is drive a few more miles away to the next church of like order to get around discipline at my "current" church, what good is the initial act of discipline which is intended for my correction and assistance? If my Reformed Baptist Church does not honor the discipline of the Reformed Baptist Church across town, how can it be said we are partners in ministry, sister churches laboring in the same vineyard for the same Lord? These are issue we must consider well, but in considering them, we must do so first and foremost with a mind to honoring Christ's lordship over His church and seeking His approval, not the approval of man. So often, as we have seen, having His approval will mean we will lose the approbation of men in Western culture today.

# CHAPTER THIRTEEN

## Warranty Fraud

For by grace you have been saved through faith; and that not
of yourselves, *it is* the gift of God; [9] not as a result of works,
so that no one may boast. [10] For we are His workmanship,
created in Christ Jesus for good works, which God prepared
beforehand so that we would walk in them (Ephesians 2:8-10).

God's grace. It is His to exercise freely, sovereignly, as He sees fit.
It cannot be demanded, it cannot be extorted from Him, otherwise it
is no longer grace. Faith in Christ. How is it related to grace? What
does it mean to trust in Christ? And how do these two concepts
relate to good works? Do they provide the foundation upon which
good works are performed, or are good works complementary to
them? In this great text the Apostle explains the relationship
between grace, faith and good works, and in so doing settled, for
those with ears to hear, centuries worth of controversy. But as we
have seen, tradition is a strong, deceptive force, and it closes ears to
the truth of God. So though Paul and provided the truth with clarity,
his words are often hidden from sight either by contrary tradition, or,
in the case of many today, a preconceived rejection of the canon of
Christian Scripture.[4]

Most of the attention paid to the relationship of grace, faith, and

---

[4] I refer to the fact that many in academia reject Pauline authorship of
Ephesians, Colossians, and the Pastoral epistles, and hence create a view of
Pauline theology that is foreign to those who read the full orbed canon of the
Christian Scriptures.

works in the history of the church has focused on whether good works are necessary to *gain* salvation. That is, is God's grace insufficient to save outside of the free human addition of works? The great Reformation conflict over *sola gratia* (grace alone) and *sola fide* (faith alone) goes to this very subject. Evangelical Protestants have historically affirmed, as part of the very definition of the gospel, the supremacy of grace and the necessity of faith. They have likewise taught that the relationship between grace, faith, and good works, has been laid out in passages such as this one in Ephesians. God's grace is first, and is hence to be praised for eternity. By grace God saves and grants to His elect saving faith in Christ. The new creature, created in the image of Christ, will, by nature, do those good works which are pleasing to His Lord, those that, to use Paul's language, God prepared beforehand that the redeemed should walk therein. Grace saves, raising to spiritual life and regenerating. Faith and repentance are gifts given to the soul that has been freed from slavery to sin and raised to spiritual life, gifts completely in harmony with God's purpose in conforming the redeemed to the image of Christ. As a result of being made a new creature in Christ, given a whole new set of longings and desires, those who are the objects of God's grace walk in newness of life, in the realm of good works, those works which God had before ordained for them. Grace brings about faith, and together these lay the foundation for a life of good works which flow from the changed nature. The good works do not add to God's grace, and God's grace is not dependent upon them, but instead powerfully produces them.

While it is not our intent to enter fully into the debate here, just one more passage should be noted before we look at a truly ancient, yet thoroughly modern as well, pulpit crime. One of the most often overlooked[5] yet definitional passages regarding the purpose of God in the gospel is found in Paul's epistle to Titus:

> For the grace of God has appeared, bringing salvation to all men, [12] instructing us to deny ungodliness and worldly desires and to live sensibly, righteously and godly in the present age, [13] looking for the blessed hope and the appearing of the glory of our great God and Savior, Christ Jesus, [14] who gave

---

[5] In modern times this would be due primarily to the rejection of Pauline authorship of Titus.

Himself for us to redeem us from every lawless deed, and to purify for Himself a people for His own possession, zealous for good deeds (Titus 2:11-14).

Two elements of this text need to be heard with clarity as the background to how important our current pulpit crime really is for the people of God: first, the grace that saves (not just makes salvation possible, but actually saves) has appeared to all men,[6] and grace that saves also teaches. You cannot split God's grace up so that it can save, but not teach. And what does it teach? It teaches those it saves to deny ungodliness and worldly desires on the negative side, and positively, it teaches us to live sensibly, righteously and godly in the present age. If a person is not taught to live in this fashion then there is every reason to question whether they have actually encountered God's saving grace, or just a facsimile thereof.

Next we have the direct scriptural assertion that the very reason for Christ's act of self-sacrifice was "to redeem us from every lawless deed, and to purify Himself a people for His own possession, zealous for good deeds." The two actions noted are "redeem" and "purify," and in both instances, Christ is the one acting in kingly power. He does not redeem or purify a theoretical group, but "us," a particular people (the elect). The unity between the two divine acts must be maintained Just as certainly as Christ's purpose was to redeem us from every lawless deed, so too His purpose is to purify for Himself a people for His own possession. Those people are described as being "zealous for good deeds." It is not their zeal for good deeds that draws to them the grace and mercy of God: instead, God's grace and mercy in Christ brings to them redemption and purification which results in their being zealous for good deeds. The changed nature longs to please Christ, and hence shows zeal to do that which pleases Him.

### Deceiving the Sheep

The Apostle John, most probably writing very late in the first century, knew of the danger posed by those who divorced the purpose of God in salvation from the act itself, separating grace and

---

[6] Logically here, as in 1 Timothy 2, Paul is speaking about all *kinds* of men, rulers, slaves, men, women, Jews, Gentiles.

its resultant work in the life of the one saved. He warns in 1 John 2:26 of those who were seeking to deceive them, to lead them astray. He goes on to say,

> No one who abides in Him sins; no one who sins has seen Him or knows Him. Little children, make sure no one deceives you; the one who practices righteousness is righteous, just as He is righteous; the one who practices sin is of the devil (3:6-8).

If you tell the people of God that those who practice unrighteousness are in fact righteous, you are deceiving them. You are engaging in false teaching. John makes it plain, here, and throughout his epistle, that there is a consistency between those who know God and their behavior. You can recognize them from what they do and how they act (the same theme struck by James in his own epistle). If they say they love God, but hate the brethren, they are liars. If they say they love God, but love the world, they are liars. And if they do not practice righteousness, they are not of God (3:10). These are not complex or difficult statements. They are not obscure or hard to understand. If you live like the devil you don't know God. Is that really that hard to understand?

Evidently, for some popular "evangelical" teachers, these statements are indeed difficult to comprehend, for they are perpetrators of a most serious pulpit crime, warranty fraud. They warranty a person's salvation, but, they do so fraudulently. Here is the current teaching.

Salvation is by faith and faith alone. Faith, for these teachers, is a very specific, but very limited, thing. It involves simple mental assent to the most basic facts about who Jesus was. All one must do is believe in Jesus for eternal life, and at that point, the transaction is sealed and finished. There is no repentance. There is no turning from sin, sorrow for sin, or anything of the kind. And what is more, you can stop right at that point, never progress any farther, never grow in the grace and knowledge of Christ, never become a disciple, a follower, never practice righteousness or love your brother or anything of the kind. In fact, if you wish, you can deny Christ, become an atheist, Buddhist, Muslim, Sikh, or maybe wander off and become a child molester or axe murderer. It really doesn't matter!

You have your ticket punched, and all that discipleship, take up your cross, live a godly life stuff shouldn't bother you at all, since, of course, that is just for super-Christians anyway! Faith alone! That's all you need.

It should be noted that when the Reformers used the phrase "faith alone" they never, *ever* meant *that* kind of faith, which is mere empty profession, surely not the faith that saves. Note, for example, the words of the Formula of Concord, III, Negative V: "We repudiate…that faith is such a confidence in the obedience of Christ as can abide and even have a being in that man who is void of true repentance…but contrary to conscience perseveres in sins." The Heidelberg Catechism, question 87 asks, "Can they, then, not be saved who do not turn to God from their unthankful, impenitent life?" The answer given is "By no means." John Calvin spoke for the Reformers in general when he stated,

> For since pardon and forgiveness are offered by the preaching of the Gospel, in order that the sinner, delivered from the tyranny of Satan, the yoke of sin, and the miserable bondage of iniquity, may pass into the kingdom of God, it is certain that no man can embrace the grace of the Gospel without retaking himself from the errors of his former life into the right path, and making it his whole study to practice repentance. (Calvin, *Institutes*, III:3:1)

So it is a gross caricature of the Reformation slogan *sola fide* to turn it to *nuda fide*, faith without substance, faith without the proper object, faith without personal relationship, faith without the work of the Spirit in the life, faith to no end but simplistic fire insurance. This is not the *sola fide* of the Reformation, the *sola fide* of the New Testament.

The strongest antidote to this shallow easy-believism is a thoroughly biblical view of the gospel as the self-glorifying work of God. Man-centered gospels are easily perverted. The God-centeredness of the biblical gospel is a strong tower against those who would seek to pervert it. God has a purpose in saving in the manner He saves. As we saw in Titus, God has a purpose in redeeming a people in Christ Jesus, and it includes their being conformed to the image of Christ, living a pure and holy life to His glory. The idea that all God is doing is throwing out a lifeline, seeking to grab as many as He can, hoping, wishing, trying, but often failing, all dependent upon the will of the creature man, leads directly to this kind of false teaching. This "Jesus will be your Savior but He surely does not need to be your Lord" kind of teaching is thoroughly man-centered. It leaves no basis for the glorification of God in the gospel. God is denied His sovereign rights to have a purpose in the great work of redemption. He is reduced to a dispenser of fire insurance policies whose highest purpose is helping briefly interested individuals to escape a nasty end, but nothing more. This is a caricature, at best, of the gospel, and it brings great disrepute upon the truth.

Sadly, many "big names" have adopted this false teaching, and have promoted it with impunity in books, study Bibles, and in the Christian media. They labor hard to defend their views. Their primary means of doing so is to create different classes of Christians. You have "regular Christians" who have been saved by the hat-tip to Jesus. What they do the rest of their lives is irrelevant, for it is not God's purpose to conform them to the image of Christ, nor is it His will that they should practice righteousness. And then there are disciples, super-serious Christians who go the extra mile. By creating this artificial distinction that has no basis at all in the inspired Scriptures (Jesus did not say "take up your cross only if you find it convenient"), they are able to dismiss the plethora of passages that so plainly identify their position as utter falsehood by saying, "Oh, those are just about those who wish to be disciples." By dismissing all the calls to holiness that are addressed to *all* believers as if they are only for *some*, these false teachers offer consolation and encouragement to those who should be following Paul's advice, "Test yourselves to see if you are in the faith; examine yourselves!" (1 Cor. 13:5). Instead, these teachers directly instruct their followers to disobey the apostolic command! Through horrific eisegesis and circular reasoning they rob their followers of the correctives of the Word of God, leading many to join the group who will hear these horrific words:

> "Many will say to Me on that day, 'Lord, Lord, did we not prophesy in Your name, and in Your name cast out demons, and in Your name perform many miracles?' 23 And then I will declare to them, 'I never knew you; DEPART FROM ME, YOU WHO PRACTICE LAWLESSNESS.'" (Matthew 7:22-23).

Please do not be deceived! The Lord clearly connected the very things these false teachers divide: He says He never knew them, and then, when He describes them, He says they "practiced lawlessness." Is this not what John said? If you practice righteousness, you know God, but, if you do not, you are lying when you say you know God. The person who is misled by these teachers into believing he or she will be saved by a gospel that leaves you unchanged, in love with your sin, enchanted by the world, will face nothing but God's wrath in the Day of Judgment. The combination of a human-centered gospel with a perversion of the meaning of faith is eternally fatal, and is one of the greatest pulpit crimes of our day.

# CHAPTER FOURTEEN

## Where Are the Cops?

For some, just the recitation of the preceding pulpit crimes is enough to cause despair. "The situation is lost, apostasy abounds!" Well, surely, apostasy does abound, but then again, that was the case in the days of the apostle John at the end of the first century, too. In many ways, even with all that is wrong, things are better today than they have been at numerous points in the history of Christ's building of His church. Every generation has thought theirs was the worst the world had ever seen, and each has bemoaned its struggles.

If the church is filled with pulpit criminals, where are the cops? Where are the authorities who are charged with apprehending these people? Who has the duty to protect the pulpit and remove those who are abusing the sacred desk? To whom shall we look for deliverance?

The very question is, in my view, frightening, for the wrong answer can be just as dangerous if not more so than the problem. The danger lies in looking outside of God's will for solutions to problems that we know will always be a part of the church's condition. When we look at the Scriptures seriously, we see that each generation is called to fight for the purity of the gospel and the sanctity of the preaching ministry. Such warnings would be useless unless the church was going to face these issues repetitively throughout her existence.

But some become impatient with the process, impatient with God's provision for the church's task. So they begin looking around for their own solutions, grasping at authorities or solutions that the Holy Spirit has not authorized in Scripture. Sadly, many a cult and false religion has gained its start not because someone was actually looking to begin a whole new religion, but because they wanted to reform the one they were in, but they did so by going outside of Scriptural boundaries. Once they established a source of authority outside of Scripture so as to get rid of abuses, those sources themselves become abusive and a source of even more falsehood! And so the cycle goes down through history. By assuming the church was supposed to somehow be freed from her struggle for purity and sound doctrine, more impurity and false doctrine is introduced.

We have already seen the provision God has provided for His people. We saw in Acts 20 and 2 Timothy 3 that in the midst of warning about false teachers and difficult times, God directed us through the Apostle to His Word and to His grace. These are our sources, our foundations, for the work of ministry, even in the midst of trial and difficulty. They are sufficient, but their very nature means they are not instantaneous in their impact. Heretics do not generally drop dead upon the first utterance of their heresy. Rarely are false teachers struck blind when they try to oppose the gospel. Instead, men of God consistently speak the truth, teach the people of God, model discernment, and are thus themselves sanctified as well as assisting in bringing about the sanctification of others. Might there be times when, from our perspective, the truth does not win out? Surely. All wars are made up of battles, and no long war has ever seen one side win all the battles. This is especially true when God's judgment comes upon a culture: from the perspective of the trenches, it looks like a *lot* of the battles are going the wrong way when judgment is falling. But in that situation, the soldiers are called to be faithful to their calling, trusting that those in charge know well their situation.

## King Jesus

Jesus Christ is the king of His church. Ultimately, it is His work, His will being accomplished. All power is His, all authority is His, and the gates of Hades itself will not stop His church in its triumphal march. As these things are true, it does not follow that in every place, at every time, His truth will be supreme. According to His purpose, and in His providence, at times His church experiences difficulty and hardship. Today, Christ's people suffer at the hands of communists and Muslims in dark lands across the globe. Why? We will someday know, I believe, but it is not ours to demand such knowledge now. But it is likewise true that in many lands where the church once marked every aspect of the culture, she is now a small minority, hardly noticed at all. Yet, at the same time, in other lands where hardly a single Christian existed a hundred years ago, thriving churches now exist. We can only but see a small piece at any one time of the entire mural of Christ's work in building His church. But just as we trust Him for our salvation, so we trust Him to do all things well.

Christ sees all that takes place in His church, and He sees as well all that takes place in those places that only pretend to be the church, but instead are dark caverns of spiritual death. He will reward His faithful servants with His presence in this life, and His "well done" in the next. But He will stand as a great judge over those who have abused His people and turned His pulpits into places of falsehood and self-aggrandizement. A great day of reckoning is coming when all will be set aright and justice will be done. No pulpit criminal has ever escaped His notice, none will escape His justice. The divine Judge will sit upon the seat of judgment, and all pulpit crime will receive its proper sentence.

## Getting the Ministry Right

But till that day, what can we as the people of God do? There is much we can do! One does not have to be an elder in a position of leadership to do something positive for the ministry of the pulpit in Christ's church. No indeed.

The first thing we can do is get the ministry right. Get our thinking about what we are doing in the church, our purpose, our calling, straight. This is true both of those in ministry, and those attending to it. For those in the ministry, our study of just some of the texts given in the Bible relating to the high calling of ministry has provided us with vital insights into what the ministry is, should be, and simply *cannot be*. So much of pulpit crime would be taken care of if we would just allow God to be God and allow His word to speak with final authority. All the false expectations, all the ungodly denominational pressures, all the worldly ideas, would be taken away and the minister would be free to do what he has been gifted and called to do.

Specifically, we need to get a clear idea of what the church is about. As long as we do not see God's purpose in building the church, the centrality of worship, the role of the word, we will keep producing the perfect environment for the promulgation of pulpit crime. Many of the errors we have examined have come about because the church was being formed into something the Spirit never intended, a hybrid, or worse, a mutation, of God's purposes. To meet these unbiblical expectations foreign elements have to be brought in, things not provided for by God's Spirit. The result is always the same. So, if we will refuse to give in to the pressures to conform the church to some other paradigm, some other vision, we will go a long way in the reduction of pulpit crime.

But the non-elder, the "layperson," has much he or she can do to battle pulpit crime. I am not referring to becoming the elder's worst nightmare, the never-satisfied critic who picks upon every perceived imperfection. Just the opposite. One of the greatest things the lay person can come to realize is their vital role in the worship of the church. By coming to the gathering of the body prepared, expectant, ready to hear from God and bless others, we add to the worship immeasurably. How often do we rob ourselves of blessings, and those around us as well, because we stumble into God's presence almost by accident rather than approaching Him with purpose and preparation! One of the most encouraging things we can do is to support the elder in his ministry of the word. Yes, by praying for him, encouraging him, but also in the very tangible way of *regularly attending to the ministry of the Word!* Every elder may claim that the number of folks in the pews does not impact him, but that is untrue. We are all humans, and when we labor to bring forth the best message we can, and yet only a few show up to hear us, we will not be encouraged. Regular attendance is not only vital to our own growth and discipleship, it is a positive ministry we should take joy from! If we expect God's regular blessings in our lives, surely we should not return to Him nothing but a hit-or-miss attitude.

Even in the worship service itself, as the Scriptures are being expounded and applied, we can have a role of encouragement. Believe me, a minister knows who is tuned in, and who is tuned out.

Nodding heads that are not saying "amen" but instead "zzzzzz" do not make the man in the pulpit work all the harder. We should often pray that God would help us with the "work of worship," and protect us from distraction and the dullness of mind that so often overtakes us. We are blessed when we concentrate upon the exposition, and the minister is blessed when he sees that we are there with a serious desire to learn and to grow in obedience.

The layperson can also greatly aid in reducing pulpit crime by being one of those in the congregation that does not demand the minister take on every possible kind of extraneous task and role. The apostles began the diaconate ministry so that they could focus upon their labor in doctrine and teaching (Acts 6:2). When we demand that the man of God in the church juggle every hat from janitor to child entertainer to program manager to IT guy to fix-it man to counselor, we are hardly going to be allowing him any ability to focus upon his own self-improvement as an exegete, let alone his preparation for his main task of leading us to the throne of God through the exposition of God's truth. Lay people can, through their freely giving of themselves, zealously protect their elders from such abuse. And what a blessing it is when they do so! Then the elders are free to follow the call of God upon their lives and actually seek to improve in their skills, become better exegetes, read more widely, and in so doing, bless the people of God more and more. The cycle can either be an upward one, with the people being more and more committed to service and the protection of the centrality of the pulpit ministry, and the elders benefiting thereby and hence blessing the people more and more in their teaching, or, it can be a downward one, with the people demanding more and more and the elders having less and less time for the proper functioning of the ministry and their own self-improvement in their Christian walk.

While these things may seem small and minor in comparison with the pulpit crimes we have examined, they are truly major means of curbing the rampant increase in pulpit crime.

## A Final Word of Encouragement

It has truly been my desire that this brief, fast-moving look at the pulpit, its proper uses, and its sinful abuses, would be an encouragement to my fellow elders, and to those precious Christian people who are concerned about God's truth. For some I hope this little book has been a swift kick in the pants, a reminder that we really do not have it all that bad, and that we cannot wallow in self-pity, since we serve a mighty Lord, and it remains a high privilege and calling to do so! For those who have not fallen into the slough of despond, but who feel the weight of discouragement because your heart is troubled by the things you see around you, hopefully just knowing that you are not, in fact, alone, will be an encouragement to you. God is not done with His church or His faithful people. He has not abandoned us. The Bible is still true, the gospel still changes lives, and it is still our privilege to lead God's people in worship before His throne. Do not allow the abuses of others to rob you of your joy! You are an ambassador of the King, gifted and called. Rejoice in your salvation, your calling, knowing that you serve the risen Lord, who will never fail to keep His own.

## OTHER SGCB TITLES

*The Origin of Paul's Religion* by J. Gresham Machen was the first book written by one of the leading apologists of the early 20th century.

*Notes on Galatians* by J. Gresham Machen is a reprint that is long overdue, especially in light of the present-day battle of the doctrine articulated in Galatians.

*Opening Scripture: A Hermeneutical Manual* by Patrick Fairbairn is a favorite volume of Sinclair Ferguson. Once again you will find help in these long-buried pages to combat many errors in today's church.

*Biblical and Theological Studies* by the professors of Princeton Seminary in 1912, at the centenary celebration of the Seminary. Articles are by men like Allis, Vos, Warfield, Machen, Wilson and others.

*Theology on Fire: Vols. 1 & 2* by Joseph A. Alexander is the two volumes of sermons by this brilliant scholar from Princeton Seminary.

*A Shepherd's Heart* by James W. Alexander is a volume of outstanding expository sermons from the pastoral ministry of one of the leading preachers of the 19th century.

*Evangelical Truth* by Archibald Alexander is a volume of practical sermons intended to be used for Family Worship.

*The Lord of Glory* by Benjamin B. Warfield is one of the best treatments of the doctrine of the Deity of Christ ever written. Warfield is simply masterful.

*The Power of God unto Salvation* by Benjamin B. Warfield is the first book of sermons ever published of this master-theologian. Several of these are found no where else.

*Mourning a Beloved Shepherd* by Charles Hodge and John Hall is a little volume containing the funeral addresses for James W. Alexander. Very informative and challenging.

**Call us Toll Free at 1-877-666-9469**
**Send us an e-mail at sgcb@charter.net**
**Visit us on line at solid-ground-books.com**

# John Eadie Titles

Solid Ground is delighted to announce that we have republished several volumes by John Eadie, gifted Scottish minister. The following are in print:

*Commentary on the Greek Text of Paul's Letter to the Galatians*
Part of the classic five-volume set that brought world-wide renown to this humble man, Eadie expounds this letter with passion and precision. In the words of Spurgeon, "This is a most careful attempt to ascertain the meaning of the Apostle by painstaking analysis of his words."

*Commentary on the Greek Text of Paul's Letter to the Ephesians*
Spurgeon said, "This book is one of prodigious learning and research. The author seems to have read all, in every language, that has been written on the Epistle. It is also a work of independent criticism, and casts much new light upon many passages."

*Commentary on the Greek Text of Paul's Letter to the Philippians*
Robert Paul Martin wrote, "Everything that John Eadie wrote is pure gold. He was simply the best exegete of his generation. His commentaries on Paul's epistles are valued highly by careful expositors. Solid Ground Christian Books has done a great service by bringing Eadie's works back into print."

*Commentary on the Greek Text of Paul's Letter to the Colossians*
According to the New Schaff-Herzog Encyclopedia of Religious Knowledge, "These commentaries of John Eadie are marked by candor and clearness as well as by an evangelical unction not common in works of the kind." Spurgeon said, "Very full and reliable. A work of utmost value."

*Commentary on the Greek Text of Paul's Letters to the Thessalonians*
Published posthumously, this volume completes the series that has been highly acclaimed for more than a century. Invaluable.

*Paul the Preacher: A Popular and Practical Exposition of His Discourses and Speeches as Recorded in the Acts of the Apostles*
Very rare volume intended for a more popular audience, this volume begins with Saul's conversion and ends with Paul preaching the Gospel of the Kingdom in Rome. It perfectly fills in the gaps in the commentaries. Outstanding work!

*DIVINE LOVE: A Series of Doctrinal, Practical and Experimental Discourses*
Buried over a hundred years, this volume consists of a dozen complete sermons from Eadie's the pastoral ministry. "John Eadie, the respected nineteenth-century Scottish Secession minister-theologian, takes the reader on an edifying journey through this vital biblical theme." - Ligon Duncan

*Lectures on the Bible to the Young for Their Instruction and Excitement*
"Though written for the rising generation, these plain addresses are not meant for mere children. Simplicity has, indeed, been aimed at in their style and arrangement, in order to adapt them to a class of young readers whose minds have already enjoyed some previous training and discipline." – Author's Preface

**Call us Toll Free at 1-877-666-9469**
**Send us an e-mail at sgcb@charter.net**
**Visit us on line at solid-ground-books.com**

CPSIA information can be obtained
at www.ICGtesting.com
Printed in the USA
BVHW071742040119
537055BV00002B/170/P